SPALDING®

I CAN do

GYMNASTICS

Essential Skills for Beginning Gymnasts

W9-BUI-503

United States Gymnastics Federation

MASTERS PRESS

A Subsidiary of Howard W. Sams & Co.

This copy of *I CAN DO GYMNASTICS*
Essential Skills for Beginning Gymnasts
Belongs to:

Name _____

Street Address _____

City, State, Zip _____

Telephone Number (____)_____

Date _____ Birthdate _____

Age _____ Grade in School _____

My Coaches are _____
_____
_____

My Club is _____

Published by Masters Press (a subsidiary of Howard W. Sams)
2647 Waterfront Pkwy E. Dr., Suite 300
Indianapolis, IN 46214

Library of Congress Cataloging-in-Publication Data

I Can do gymnastics : essential skills for beginning gymnasts / The United
    States Gymnastics Federation.
        p.   cm. — (Spalding sports library)
    Summary: Instructions for developing skills in the beginning gymnast.
        ISBN 0-940279-51-7 : $12.95
    1. Gymnastics for children—juvenile literature.
    [1. Gymnastics.] I. United States Gymnastics Federation. II. Series.
GV464.5.I5   1992   92-2441
796.44'083—dc20   CIP
                                                                          AC

Credits:

    Cover design by Lynne Annette Clark and Michelle Lambert

    Text design by Leah Marckel

    Edited by Holly Witten Kondras

Table of Contents

Acknowledgments

Special thanks to the authors and editors of *Sequential Gymnastics II*, the basis for this book:

Patty Hacker, South Dakota State University, Brookings, SD

Eric Malmerg, State University College, Cortland, NY

Jim Nance, University of Kentucky, Lexington, KY

Alan Tilove, National School Assemblies, Valencia, CA

Susan True, National Federation of State High School Associations, Kansas City, MO

Terry Exner, GymMarin, San Rafael, CA

Steve Whitlock, Director of Educational Services and Safety, U.S. Gymnastics Federation, Indianapolis, IN

Dave Moskovitz, Coaching Development Coordinator, U.S. Gymnastics Federation, Indianapolis, IN

Thanks also to James Stephenson, Georges McKail, and Lynn Wilton for their wonderful illustrations in the text, and to the Australian Gymnastics Federation for permission to reproduce selected skills from the *GYM FUN* series.

Thanks to Steve Calisch of Calisch Photography and the coaches and gymnasts at Terry Spencer's World of Gymnastics for their assistance with the photographs in the text.

How to Use this Program

I Can Do Gymnastics: Essential Skills for Beginning Gymnasts was adapted from the U.S.G.F.'s *Sequential Gymnastics II: An Instructors Guide*. The purpose of these activities is to expand the movement vocabulary of children through sequential gymnastics presented in a safe and fun enveronment.

Safety is the most important aspect of any gymnastics program. Safety considerations are built into the skilll sequences included in this book. The athletes progress through the program skill by skill, each building on the last. The skills should be learned as listed in progressive order, beginning with Level of Difficulty: A, skill 1.

The activities in each movement category, (for example, Backward Rolling Skills), are internalized by the students before progressing to the next skill. Internalizing a skill means that the student can perform the skill easily in a fluent, spontaneous manner. This insures that the gymnast is always ready to move to the next skill and is confident in his/her ability to perform.

The student can record his or her progress by checking each skill sequence as it is mastered in the summary chart at the end of each chapter.

I Can Do Gymnastics can serve as a helpful guideline for the parents of beginning gymnasts. Parents can learn about the sport of gymnastics and gymnastics terminology while monitoring the progress or their children. The program is effective only when used in the proper setting and by people with the appropriate training to teach and train young gymnasts — professional gymnastics teachers and coaches. The role of the parents is to help motivate, set goals, and encourage their child's interest in gymnastics.

Steve Whitlock
Director of Educational Services and Safety

Equipment

In gymnastics, the equipment you use is very important. You should always make sure that when you practice your gymnastic skills that you do so in a safe environment and with the right equipment. Here is a list of the equipment you will use with your coach in the gym.

GYM EQUIPMENT:

Panel Mats: These come in assorted sizes and colors. The size you will probably use is 5 by 10 feet or 6 by 12 feet. The color will be different from the ceiling, walls, and floor so that you can always see where the mat is, even when doing skills upside-down, backwards, and sideways.

Wedge (Incline Mat): The recommended size is 5 by 6 feet and 18 to 20 inches high.

Single Bar: Your first bar skills will be performed on a low horizontal bar that adjusts from 3 to 5 feet high. How high the bar is set will depend on your *height* not on your ability.

Springboard: Junior or regulation size is appropriate for the beginning gymnast.

Balance Beam: Adjustable height from low (6 inches) to medium (12 to 24 inches), covered with a padded or nonslip surface. Equipment should only be used with appropriate matting.

Rope: Ropes will range from between 5 and 10 inches, be sure to use the size that is best for you. The ends of the rope should be knotted.

Hoops: Plastic hoops should be from 24 to 28 inches in diameter. They should be wrapped with plastic tape to prevent warping and bending.

Balls: Plastic balls should be between 5 and 8 inches around. Balls should be soft and slightly under-inflated. You should be able to hold the ball comfortably with one hand.

Ribbons: Ribbons should be made of nylon-satin material, between 6 and 16 feet long, and attached to the end of a fiberglass stick. The stick should between 15 and 24 inches long and the ribbon will be held on by a small ring. Make sure that both the ribbon and the stick are not too long for you.

There are some skills in this book that you will be able to practice at home. For example, the rhythmic gymnastics skills can be practiced almost anywhere. Make sure that you have your coach's OK before you practice outside the gym so that you run the least chance of getting hurt.

For the Gymnast

I *Can Do Gymnastics: Essential Skills for Beginning Gymnasts* is a step by step way for you to learn new gymnastics skills. Each chapter will start with the easiest skill in that area of gymnastics and build up to harder skills. Each skill builds on the skill before it, so be sure that you can really do a skill well by yourself before you move up to the next skill.

Always start with A level skills and skill number 1 when you begin a section. Just because you think you know how to do a skill already doesn't mean you know how to do it the safest and the best way. If you progress from one skill to the next and get checked on each skill by your coach as you go through each level, you will be sure to be learning the skills the right way. This causes less problems later on.

This book is really designed to go with the gymnastics program at your club or school. Most require special equipment and assistance that only a professional coach and club will have. You will need help on a lot of these skills when you start doing them because you could get hurt trying to do them without proper help from a professional gymnastics coach. Your coach will know the best way to "spot" you on a skill. Gyms also usually have all the right type of equipment in your size, and with the right type of mats and other safety equipment in case you fall.

However, there are skills that you can always practice at home. As a gymnast you need to work on becoming stronger and improving your coordination and flexibility. The rhythmic skills in the last chapter of this book can be done almost anywhere, once you know the basics and have the right equipment. You will need to practice the skills in chapter one, *Learning to Fall*, many, many times, until they become completely natural to you.

Remember: the most important thing to think about in gymnastics is your safety. If you are ever scared or don't think you can do a trick, tell your coach. Your coach will make sure that everything will be done to make you feel safe and prepared to complete every skill.

For the Parent

Who can do gymnastics?

Everyone!

I Can Do Gymnastics: Essential Skills for Beginning Gymnasts presents the skills that are the building blocks for human movement through the sport of gymnastics. All the skills necessary for each child to develop body awareness and control are presented in a simple and safe way with plenty of illustrations to demonstrate each skill.

I Can Do Gymnastics was adapted from and intended to accompany the *Sequential Gymnastics II* program for skill development. *Sequential II* was designed by a team of physical education experts to teach gymnastics skills to youth and beginning gymnasts in the most effective, efficient, and safe ways possible. This book should be used as a tool to help the gymnast chart his or her progress in gymnastics and to help the parent develop an understanding gymnastics. Training of the actual skills should only be attempted by a qualified gymnastics coach.

Encourage your child's participation in gymnastics, for it is an excellent way for a young person to acquire overall physical fitness, poise, confidence, and self discipline. However, make sure that the gymnast always practices the skills learned in a safe supervised setting.

If you want to learn more about gymnastics and share in your children's success as they progress through the sport then you have selected a very helpful tool to add to your personal library. Enjoy!

Rik Feeney
Gymnastics Coach and Author *Gymnastics: A Guide for Parents and Athletes*

1

Learning to Fall

Falling and landing skills are the most important skills to learn in the sport of gymnastics. If you practice these basic drills until you land using the basic safety landing position every time, you can use the safety skills when you aren't practicing gymnastics. You will be less likely to get hurt when playing other sports with your friends, or on the playground, or anywhere else!

When you are first learning the following safety drills make sure you are practicing them under the supervision of your coach. Your coach will make sure that you are learning how to land and fall correctly.

SAFETY LANDING DRILLS

The basic safety landing drills are:

1. **Basic Safety Landing Position (or SLP):** The basic position to land from a skill is to stand mostly upright with the arms up next to the ears (to help protect the neck and head), the knees bent to a 45 degree angle, the stomach sucked in, weight on the balls of the feet (not flat-footed or on the toes), and the lower back slightly rounded.

It is important to remember that the back is always rounded and the knees are bent on landing, otherwise the force of the landing can severely jar your lower back, possibly causing injury.

Note: When practicing these Safety Landing Drills, always begin from a low surface such as a folded-up mat and progressively work up to a higher surface such as a balance beam. Don't jump off anything that is higher than your waist.

No matter which basic landing drill you are practicing always remember that you should try to land on your feet first!

Basic SLP

SLP with Side Roll

2. **SLP with a Side Roll:** This safety landing is especially for if you over-rotate when you are landing. To practice: Lay on the mat on your back and bring both knees up to your chest. Roll completely over in a sideways direction. Next: Practice landing in SLP then going into a sideways roll. Practice rolling to both sides.

I CAN DO GYMNASTICS

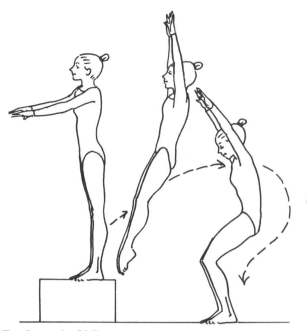

Note: When you start practicing this skill, you may want to grab your knees to do the side roll. Remember that you should keep your arms up to protect your head and practice the skill that way.

3. **Backwards SLP:** This is the same as the basic SLP except that you are landing with rotation in a backward direction.

Note: Be sure that when you practice jumping backwards you keep your head up. Many gymnasts have a tendency to look down which causes them to strike their head on the equipment they are jumping from. Remember to always work up from lower to higher platforms in practicing these skills.

4. **Backwards SLP with Tuck and Roll:** Lay on the floor knees and hips bent, lower back rounded, arms up above the head. Practice rocking back and forth in this position.

Next, jump off a raised surface landing in Backwards SLP, and continue through to the floor rocking backwards (without going over) then rolling back up to a stand. Do not roll over all the way as it is very easy to compress the neck in this position.

Try to remember to always protect the head, neck, and back first when you fall.

Hand Position: When over-rotating a landing the hands may be placed on the ground to help guide the body into the roll which will break the force of the fall. The hands should not be used to catch the entire body weight during a fall. Practice closing fists when you fall from the apparatus so that you will not try to roll or break a fall with a partially open hand.

Backwards SLP with Tuck and Roll

Falling Backwards: Never place the arms behind the body with the elbows locked as this invites serious injury to the wrist and elbow, or possible dislocation of the shoulder. If the hands are placed on the floor during a backwards rotating fall, the hands should be placed at the sides of the body with the fingers pointing towards the toes so that the elbows can bend as the body rolls backwards.

Horizontal or Uneven Bars: Practice each of the drills from a small swing on the bars. Falling from a swing can be a much different experience than falling from other pieces of apparatus. A gymnast may fall off going in a forward direction while the body rotates backward or vice versa on the bars. When dismounting, you should always release the bar at the peak of your swing, not while you are still rising in the swing.

The principles for safe landings are the same for almost any sport. Landings from falling off the jungle gym onto cement are much worse than those in a gymnastics class. So learning how to fall will be helpful at the school playground or any other sporting activity you might be involved in.

Note: Initially all these skills should be practiced under the strict supervision of a qualified gymnastics coach and competent spotter.

I CAN DO GYMNASTICS

2

Across the Floor

The skills you learn on the floor are the basis for the skills you will perform on all the other apparatus in the gym. In general you will first learn how to do a skill on the floor before trying it out on the other equipment.

For example, the handstand is used in almost every event: the bars, the beam, the vault . . . although you may only be doing one for a few seconds. If you know how to do a handstand with the proper form and technique on the floor, then it will be much easier to learn how to perform a front handspring on the vault or a front walkover on the beam.

It is important for you to develop your floor skills in an orderly and progressive manner, and with a lot of attention to the basics. Every skill you learn will help you learn more difficult skills, both on the floor and in other events. Don't take shortcuts just to learn a skill for it s own sake. Learn the skills right the first time so you won't have to learn them again later to perform at higher levels. The progressions in this book were developed so that you will learn how to do the skills correctly and safely.

Gymnastics is basically a collection of skills combined together in different ways. Everything you learn, no matter how minor it seems, will lead to something else, all of which you will need to know later in developing routines. So be sure you learn how to do everything right the first time.

Floor exercise routines are performed on a mat or a special floor known as a spring floor (a springy but firm surface that helps gymnasts tumble higher and still land safely.) The floor that you will perform on measures 40 x 40 feet. The performance area is surrounded by a two-foot border, in case you should step or fall out of bounds.

I CAN DO GYMNASTICS

UPRIGHT BALANCE SKILLS ON THE MAT

Level of Difficulty: A

1  **The V-Seat** Sit on a mat, slide the feet toward the seat (tuck position with the hands on the mat next to the seat.) Lift the legs to a V position, hold momentarily, then extend and lift your hands at your sides, balance for two seconds.

2 **The Lunge** Step forward to a stand in a lunge position (knee of the front leg is bent).

What to Practice:
- Keep your head up, eyes focused forward.
- Square your shoulders.
- Extend your back leg.
- Your legs should be in a straight line perpendicular to your shoulders.
- Remember to "turn out" your feet.

3  **Arabesque** Stand on both feet, keeping you upper body vertical and extended. Lift one leg backward and upward (6″ - 12″ or higher), maintain a vertical curve in the body.

Note: For a **Scale**, the upper body is lowered (shoulders to about hip height) as the back leg is raised to the horizontal position or above.

UPRIGHT BALANCE SKILLS ON THE MAT

Level of Difficulty: B

4 Y-Scale Stand on both feet. Slowly lift one leg to your side(with control). Hold the leg with the same side hand.

> **What to practice:**
> - Keep your head up, your eyes focused forward.
> - The foot of your support leg should be flat on the floor.
> - Your base leg should be fully extended.
> - Keep your torso upright.

5 Side Scale Stand on both feet. Lift one leg to the side while at the same time lowering your upper body to the opposite side. Try to hold the leg at or above horizontal.

6 Cross Leg Hand Support Sit cross-legged on the mat with the hands beside your hips (on the mat.) Lift to a support with the seat and legs off the mat by extending the arms (the feet do not need to come off the mat on the first few attempts.)

UPRIGHT BALANCE SKILLS ON THE MAT
Level of Difficulty: C

7 **Tuck Support** Sit on the mat in a tuck position with the hands beside the hips on the mat. Lift to a support by extending the arms and attempting to lift the seat and feet off the mat.

8 **1/2 "L" Support** Perform the Tuck Support as described above, then attempt to slowly extend one leg into a pike position, keeping the other leg in a tuck position. Repeat the activity using the other leg.

9 **"L" Support** Sit in a pike position on the mat with the hands on the mat by the hips. Extend the arms to lift the seat and legs off the mat in an open pike position while maintaining a vertical position of the torso.

UPRIGHT AGILITY SKILLS ON THE MAT

Level of Difficulty: A

1 **Turns (Pirouettes)** Step forward, raising up on the ball of the front foot and turn 90, 180, or 360 degrees, to finish in various positions. Arms and free leg: optional position.

> **What to Practice:**
> - Keep head up, remember to "spot" the turn
> - Your base foot should remain on toe throughout the turn.
> - Your center of gravity should rest on base leg.
> - Keep torso upright.

2 **Stretch Jump with Twists** Jump up from mat with body in an extended (stretched) position, twist 180 or 360 degrees and land on both feet. Repeat the activity, turning in the opposite direction. Remember to land in the SLP.

3 **Hurdle** Step forward and hop off one foot while swinging the rear leg forward into another step. (This is a preparatory movement.)

Note: To do an **assemblé** lift one leg forward and upward, then push off the other leg and bring both legs together in the air. Finish by landing on both feet in a controlled position. Repeat the activity beginning with the other leg.

UPRIGHT AGILITY SKILLS ON THE MAT
Level of Difficulty: B

4 **Chassé** Step forward and spring slightly off the floor. The legs come together momentarily in the air. Land on the back leg with the front leg lifted slightly in preparation for the next movement. Repeat the activity moving to the side both on the right and the left.

5 **Hitchkick** Step forward and push off the front foot while swinging the back leg forward and upward. Switch the leg positions in the air and land on the back leg.

6 **Sissone** Step forward and place the back foot forward to a position behind the front foot. Jump and separate the legs to a stride position. Land on the front leg in a low arabesque.

UPRIGHT AGILITY SKILLS ON THE MAT

Level of Difficulty: C

 Stride Leap From a slow run forward, push off one foot to rise in the air, separate the legs to a stride position, and land on the front foot with the knee slightly bent. Repeat the activity pushing off the other leg.

Foutté Step forward, swing the back leg forward and upward, then spring slightly off the support leg and execute a 180 degree turn landing in a low arabesque on the push-off leg.

 Tourjeté Step forward, swing the back leg forward and upward, then spring slightly off the base leg and execute a 180 degree turn while switching the legs landing in a low arabesque on the leg which was first lifted in the air.

What to Practice:

- Make sure your kick forward is powerful to start the leap.
- Keep turn sharp.
- Leg kick backward must be powerful when switching legs.
- Keep head and torso up when landing.

FORWARD ROLLING SKILLS ON THE WEDGE

Level of Difficulty: A

1
Log Roll Up/Down Mat Begin in a supine position on the upper end of the wedge with the body fully extended, then roll over into a prone position and continue rolling to the end of the wedge. Repeat the activity rolling back up the wedge, and rolling in the opposite direction.

2 **Slide Off Forward Roll** Begin in a prone position with the head toward the high end of the wedge and slide forward placing the hands on the mat next to the wedge. With support on the arms, look at the abdomen and roll over forward off the wedge onto the mat. **Hands should be placed as close to the edge of the wedge as possible.**

3
Tip Over Forward Roll (shown with spot) Begin on the shins with arms extended high, positioned on the high end of the wedge facing away from the downslope. Reach for the mat with the hands, look at the stomach and roll over forward to finish in a standing position on the mat. **Hands should be placed as close to the edge of the wedge as possible.**

FORWARD ROLLING SKILLS ON THE WEDGE

Level of Difficulty: B

4 **Straddle Forward Roll Down** Stand on the high edge of the wedge in a straddle position facing down the wedge. Reach between and behind the legs, place the hands on the mat to perform a forward roll to stand with feet together. **Place your upper back on the wedge at the beginning of the roll.**

5 **Tuck Forward Roll Down** From a stand, squat down on the high end of the wedge, facing down the wedge. Place the hands on the wedge in front of the feet, shoulder width apart. Raise the hips and push off the feet to perform a forward roll down the wedge. You should finish in a straight stand.

6 **Roll Up and Over** Step onto the low end of the wedge, facing the upslope of the wedge. Moving through a scale position, roll over forward up the wedge to a sitting position on the high edge of the wedge with arms extended forward. As the feet contact the mat jump upward and forward and land on two feet. Repeat the activity adding a turn, tuck, straddle, or pike to the final jump.

FORWARD ROLLING SKILLS ON THE WEDGE

Level of Difficulty: C

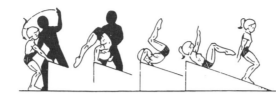

7 **Roll Over and Down (shown with spot)** Facing the high end of the wedge, place the hands on the high end of the wedge. Jump off both feet to a forward roll down the wedge finishing in a stand. A spotter may be used.

> **What to Practice:**
> - Make sure your jump is powerful.
> - Be sure to pull your chin to your chest at the beginning of the roll.
> - Try to maintain control throughout the movement.

8 **Extended Forward Roll Over and Down (shown with spot)** Run and place the hands on the high end of the wedge. Push off the feet, keeping the arms extended, and lean forward onto the wedge to perform a forward roll over the high edge and down the slope. Finish in a stretched standing position.

9 **Run — Jump — Forward Roll (shown with a spot)** Run and place the hands on the high end of the wedge, facing down the wedge. Jump from both feet, extend the legs overhead, and roll forward down the wedge. The arms should be used for support while the legs are extended.

BACKWARD ROLLING SKILLS ON THE WEDGE

Level of Difficulty: A

1 **Back Roll Down** Sit on the high end of the wedge facing away from the downslope. Roll backward with the hands beside the head. Hold the legs in a tuck position, **use the hands for support as the body becomes inverted**. Finish by pushing off the hands and extending the legs to a standing position. (This skill can be performed starting from a stand on the wedge.)

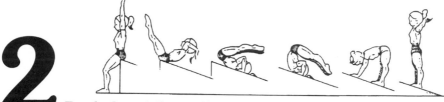

2 **Back Straddle Roll Down** Sit on the high end of the wedge facing away from the head. Straighten the legs to a straddle position, **use the hands for support as the body becomes inverted.** Finish by pushing off the hands to a straddle stand. (This skill can be performed from a stand on the wedge.)

3 **Back Roll to Straight Jump** Perform the Back Roll Down as shown above. As the legs are extending to the standing position, jump upward to land on the mat on two feet. (This skill can be performed from a stand on the wedge.)

What to Practice:
- Be sure to roll in a straight line down the wedge.
- Maintain proper hand position and support in the inverted position.
- Stay in control during the straight jump.

I CAN DO GYMNASTICS

BACKWARD ROLLING SKILLS ON THE WEDGE

Level of Difficulty: B

4 **Back/Front Roll Combinations** Sit on the high end of the wedge facing away from the downslope. Roll backward down the wedge. As the feet land, push off the hands and jump upward with an 180 degree turn landing with the back facing the wedge. Then perform a forward roll to a stand. (This skill can be performed from a stand on the wedge.)

5 **Two Back Rolls** Sit on the high end of the wedge facing away from the downslope. Roll backward down the wedge, straddling the legs to execute a straddle roll to a straddle stand. From the straddle stand, perform a back roll finishing in a stretched stand. (This skill can be performed from a stand on the wedge.)

6 **Low Back Extensions Step-Out (shown with spot)** Sit on the high end of the wedge. Roll backward down the wedge placing the hands on the wedge by the shoulders. Extend the hips and knees as the hands contact the wedge and extend the arms lifting the shoulders off the wedge. Finish by stepping down one leg at a time moving through a lunge.

BACKWARD ROLLING SKILLS ON THE WEDGE
Level of Difficulty: C

7 **Jump to Back Roll Down** Stand with the heels near the high edge of the wedge. Jump upward and backward to land in a sitting position with the feet on the mat and the seat on the wedge. Roll backward down the wedge pushing off the hands and finish in a stand.

8 **Cartwheel Jump to Back Roll Down** Perform a cartwheel finishing with the back toward the high edge of the wedge. Step back bringing the feet together. Jump upward and backward to land in a sitting position with the feet on the mat and the seat on the wedge. Roll backward down the wedge pushing off the hands and finish in a stand.

9 **Bridge Over High Edge (shown with spot)** Lie in a supine position with head toward the high edge of the wedge. Reach the hands overhead toward the mat (fingertips as close to the edge of the wedge as possible). Bridge up to support, push off with one leg while lifting the other leg overhead (walkover position), and step down to the mat.

FORWARD ROLLING SKILLS ON THE MAT

Level of Difficulty: A

1 **Tip-Over From Scale** From a controlled scale position, lean forward to place the hands on the mat. Tuck the head (chin to chest) and perform a forward roll to a standing position.

2 **Straddle/Tuck Forward Roll** From a straddle pike stand, perform a forward roll to squat position and extend the legs to a straight stand.

3 **Forward Roll Walk-Out** From a stand, place the hands on the mat, perform a forward roll. As the body rolls along the back, keep one leg tucked while the other leg extends forward slightly. Finish by rising to a stand.

What to Practice:
- Make sure the back rolls on the mat smoothly from neck to seat.
- Keep the movement from roll to stand continuous.
- Keep head up and eyes focused forward as legs push up to stand.

FORWARD ROLLING SKILLS ON THE MAT

Level of Difficulty: B

4 **Prone Forward Roll (shown with spot)** Start in a prone position on the mat, push up, dragging/walking the feet to a position as close to the head as flexibility will allow. Elevate the hips, transferring body weight to the hands and arms, tuck the head and roll over forward, finishing in a stand.

5 **Straddle Forward Roll** From a straddle stand, pike and place the hands on the mat slightly in front of the feet. Roll over forward, maintaining a straddle position, and finish in a straddle stand.

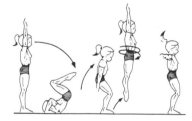

6 **Forward Roll to Jumps** From a straight stand, perform a forward roll. While rising to stand, jump and execute a stretched body jump, tuck jump, pike jump, straddle jump, or a jump with a twist.

What to Practice:
- Keep rhythm continuous throughout the activity,
- Maintain control on all jumps.
- Keep head and chest up on landing.

FORWARD ROLLING SKILLS ON THE MAT
Level of Difficulty: C

7 **Pike/Tuck Forward Roll** From a stretched standing position, legs together, pike forward to place the hands on the mat in front of the feet. Roll over forward, tucking the body when the hips touch the mat. Finish in a stand.

What to Practice:
- Make sure that you bend at the hips.
- Keep back rounded throughout the roll.
- Remember that your legs should remain straight as long as possible.

 1/2 Handstand Forward Roll From a stretched position, move though a scale (left or right foot), simultaneously place the hands on the mat and roll forward finishing in a stand. The support leg remains in contact with the mat until the back touches on the forward roll.

9 **Handstand Forward Roll** Lunge forward, bend at the hips, and place the hands on the mat. With a spot, push up though a handstand position, tuck the head, and lower to the upper back and shoulders. Roll forward to finish in a stand.

BACKWARD ROLLING SKILLS ON THE MAT

Level of Difficulty: A

1 **Roll Backward to Shoulder Balance** Begin in a sitting position, roll back to a shoulder balance position with the arms fully extended overhead. Show various balance positions — tuck pike, straddle.

2 **Straddle/Tuck Backward Roll** From a straddle stand, roll backward while at the same time reaching between the legs to assist with roll back to a sitting position. Continue rolling backward, using the arms to support the body, bring the knees together. Finish in a squat stand.

3 **Straddle Backward Roll** From a straddle position, either standing or sitting, roll backward while maintaining a straddle position. Push off the hands finishing in a straddle stand.

BACKWARD ROLLING SKILLS ON THE MAT

Level of Difficulty: B

4 **Backward Roll** From a stretched standing position, perform a backward roll to stretched standing position.

5 **Prone Backward Roll** From a prone position, push up to a front leaning support and snap to a squat position, then push off the hands and roll backward through a tuck position to a stretched standing position.

6 **Pike/Tuck Backward Roll (shown with spot)** Begin in a pike standing position, bend forward and reach backward to catch the body's weight as the roll is initiated. As the seat touches the mat continue to roll backward by tucking the knees and the arms up beside the head. Push off the hands, moving through a squat position, finishing in a stand.

BACKWARD ROLLING SKILLS ON THE MAT
Level of Difficulty: C

7 **Backward Rolls with Jumps** Perform jumps in various positions before and after a backward roll.

> **What to Practice:**
> - Be sure you regain your balance before beginning the backward roll.
> - Support yourself with the hands during the roll.
> - Maintain control during final jump and landing.

8 **Tuck/Pike Backward Roll** From a squat position, roll backward and pike to a stand.

9 **Backward Roll to Arabesque** From a stand, roll backward. As the hands make contact with the mat, extend one leg upward and backward. Extend the arms, pushing the body off the floor and lift the chest to finish in an arabesque position.

INVERTED BALANCE SKILLS ON THE MAT

Level of Difficulty: A

1 **Double Knee Up** From a squat position, form a triangle with the hands and head (head is at the top of the triangle; head touches the mat at the hairline.) Place one knee on each elbow and lift the hips to balance on the hands and forehead (TRIPOD). Slowly lift the legs to a tuck position and hold. The majority of the body weight should be supported on the hands.

2 **Headstand** Balance in a tripod as shown above, then extend both the hips and legs to balance in a extended handstand. (Head touches mat at hairline.)

What to Practice:
- Make sure your head and hands form a triangle.
- Be sure that you support and balance your body with your arms.
- Maintain control and balance throughout the skill.

3  **Headstand Roll Out** Balance in a tripod, then slowly extend the legs to balance in a stretched headstand position. After balancing, allow the legs to lean slightly forward, PUSH WITH THE HANDS to lift the head slightly off the mat, tuck the head, and roll forward through a squat position to stand.

INVERTED BALANCE SKILLS ON THE MAT

Level of Difficulty: B

4  **Prone Press to Headstand (shown with spot)** From a prone position, walk/slide/lift the legs to stretched headstand position. (Straddle the legs prior to lifting.)

5  **Single Leg Swing Up Toward Handstand** Start in a front leaning support, then lift one leg above horizontal and shift the body weight onto the arms. Push off the floor with the remaining support leg, switch leg position in the air, and lower the raised leg to finish in a front leaning support.

6  **3/4 Handstand Switch Legs** From a stand with arms high, step forward moving through a lunge, place the hands on the floor, and lift the back leg as high as possible. Keep the arms extended. Push off the base leg and switch leg position in the air lowering the first leg. Push off the hands to a lunge position and step back to a straight stand.

INVERTED BALANCE SKILLS ON THE MAT

Level of Difficulty: C

7 **Walk the Wall** From a prone position with feet against the wall, walk the feet part way up the wall while at the same time moving the hands closer to the wall. Then slowly reverse the process to return to a prone position. **Your own strength will determine how far up the wall you can go.**

8 **Piked Handstand Roll From Wall (shown with spot)** Walk the feet up the wall to a piked handstand position with the abdomen facing the wall. Push off the wall with the feet, tuck the head, and roll forward on back to a stand. **The first few times you try this, you should use an additional mat or skill cushion.**

What to Practice:

- Make sure to move your shoulders with your arms.
- Your head should not bear weight on the forward roll.
- Maintain control and balance throughout.

9 **Lift to Momentary Handstand (shown with a spot)** From a stand with arms high, lunge forward lifting the back leg while placing the hands on the floor, and push off the front leg. Bring the legs together in a straight handstand position. Hold momentary balance with assistance and step down, moving through a lunge to finish in a stand.

INVERTED AGILITY SKILLS (WHEELS)
ON THE MAT
Level of Difficulty: A

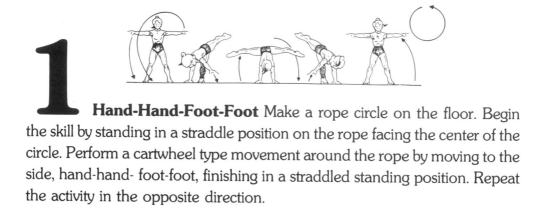

1 **Hand-Hand-Foot-Foot** Make a rope circle on the floor. Begin the skill by standing in a straddle position on the rope facing the center of the circle. Perform a cartwheel type movement around the rope by moving to the side, hand-hand- foot-foot, finishing in a straddled standing position. Repeat the activity in the opposite direction.

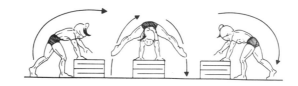

2 **1/2 Cartwheel Over Mats** From a straddle stand facing the folded mat, place the hands on the mat using the cartwheel action to move to the other side of the mat. Repeat the activity with the other foot in front.

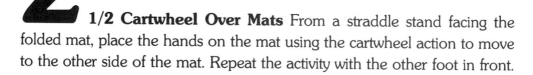

3 **Low Cartwheel Over Rope** Reach out and over a rope (12″ to 24″ high), placing the hands on the mat and push off one leg at a time using the cartwheel action to finish in straddle stand on the other side of the rope. Repeat the activity on the other side.

I CAN DO GYMNASTICS

INVERTED AGILITY SKILLS (WHEELS)
ON THE MAT

Level of Difficulty: B

4 **Downhill Cartwheel** Stand on the high end of the wedge, facing downhill. Perform a cartwheel down the wedge with control. Repeat the activity on the other side.

5 **Cartwheel (shown with spot)** From a straddle stand with arms stretched to side-middle, perform a cartwheel. Repeat the activity on the other side.

6 **Three Steps to Cartwheel** Take three walking steps, raising the arms during the third step, and perform a cartwheel as shown above. Repeat the activity on the other side.

INVERTED AGILITY SKILLS (WHEELS)
ON THE MAT

Level of Difficulty: C

7 Hurdle Cartwheel Step forward onto one foot, then hop and step forward with the other foot into a cartwheel. Repeat the activity on the other side.

8 Cartwheel Style Round Off Step forward to place the hands on the mat and perform a cartwheel. As the first leg contacts the floor, turn the body 90 degrees to face the starting point, and close the second leg to the first to finish with feet together in a stand.

9 Step Into a Round Off Step forward to place the hands on the mat as in a cartwheel. As the feet pass overhead, push off the hands, turn 90 degrees as shown above, and close the legs together quickly just before the first foot contacts the floor. Finish with knees slightly bent and body leaning backward.

What to Practice:
- Make a strong push from your front leg.
- Be sure body passes through vertical.
- Keep feet together on the landing

I CAN DO GYMNASTICS

Checklist for Floor Skills

Skill	Level of Difficulty			Date Skill Series Completed
	A	**B**	**C**	
Upright Balance				
Upright Agility				
Forward Rolling (Wedge)				
Backward Rolling (Wedge)				
Forward Rolling (Mat)				
Backward Rolling (Mat)				
Inverted Balance				
Inverted Agility (Wheels)				

3

Over the Vault

The apparatus you use when you are vaulting is called the horse. The name comes from the time that soldiers used to run and jump on or over real horses. The "regulation" horse is adjustable in height. You will probably practice vaulting skills using stacked mats, foam trapezoids, or vaulting boxes at first and then progress to the actual horse at a low setting. Advanced performers use the vault at 47.25 inches, which is almost four feet high!

The springboard you push off from is four feet long and three feet wide and slanted in design. The slant will allow you to transfer the speed built up from running down the mat to height to carry you over the horse.

Originally, men and women both used the same equipment for vaulting. As the sport progressed, changes in the events were made to show the artistic qualities of women's gymnastics and to emphasize the strength aspect of men's gymnastics. For men's gymnastics the horse is positioned for the gymnast to vault over it lengthwise. This type of vaulting is called "longhorse" vaulting. In women's gymnastics, the horse is positioned for the gymnast to vault over it sideways. Boys and girls alike, however, learn all the beginning vaulting skills with the horse sideways.

SERIES OF JUMP SKILLS ON THE VAULT

Level of Difficulty: A

For these skills, stacked panel mats (approximately 24" high) should be positioned perpendicular to the direction of motion. The vaulting board is then placed close to the front of the first mat.

1 **Jump — Jump — Tuck Jump** Run, hurdle, and rebound off the board landing on the first mat. Then jump from the first mat to the second mat and jump off the second mat bending and raising the knees to a tuck position. Extend the legs, land on the feet in the SLP before finishing in a straight stand.

2 **Jump — Jump — Straddle Jump** Begin as shown above. In the final jump, straddle the legs and attempt to touch the toes while keeping the head and chest up. Bring the legs together, land on the feet in the SLP before finishing in a straight stand.

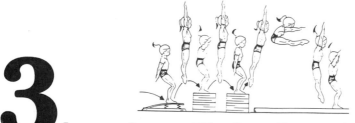

3 **Jump — Jump — Pike Jump** Begin as shown in skills above. In the final jump, pike at the hips while keeping the head and chest up. Extend at the hips to a vertical position, land on the feet in the SLP before finishing in a straight stand.

I CAN DO GYMNASTICS

SERIES OF JUMP SKILLS ON THE VAULT

Level of Difficulty: B

4 **Double Jump — Jump 180 Degree Turn** With folded panel mats and springboard spaced close together, run, hurdle and rebound off the board to land on the first mat. Then jump from the first mat to the second mat, jump off the second mat, and execute a 180 degree turn before landing on the feet in the SLP before finishing in a straight stand. Repeat the activity and turn in the opposite direction.

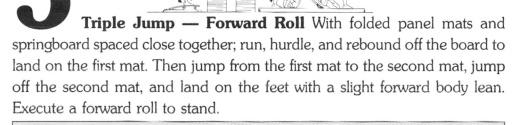

5 **Triple Jump — Forward Roll** With folded panel mats and springboard spaced close together; run, hurdle, and rebound off the board to land on the first mat. Then jump from the first mat to the second mat, jump off the second mat, and land on the feet with a slight forward body lean. Execute a forward roll to stand.

What to Practice:
- Make sure that run and hurdle are continuous.
- Execute jumps with good balance and control.
- Always demi-plié before beginning forward roll.

6 **Traveling Jumps Up and Down** With folded panel mats set end-to-end, travel forward with support on the hands by jumping from the side of the mat to the top of the mat, to the other side of the mat, back to the top, and so forth. Each time the feet have support on the floor move the hand forward 6" to 12".

SERIES OF JUMP SKILLS ON THE VAULT

Level of Difficulty: C

7

Traveling Jumps Over and Back With folded panel mats set end-to-end, travel forward with support on the hands by jumping from one side of the mat to the other side of the mat without touching the feet on the top of the mat, raising the arms for each landing.

8

Squat on, Forward Roll With the springboard close to the folded panel mats, stand on the springboard with the hands on the mat, bounce to a squat position on top on top of the mat. Forward roll on top of the folded panel mat to a stand on the mat.

9

Forward Roll on, Jump, Land, Forward Roll With the springboard close to the folded panel mat, run forward, hurdle, and rebound off the board with feet together. Place both hands on top of the folded panel mat, raise the hips and roll forward to stand on the mat. Jump off the panel mat, landing on the feet, and roll forward to a stand.

What to Practice:
- Your hips and legs should rise following board contact
- Maintain control during the forward roll on the mat
- Keep movement continuous throughout the activity

I CAN DO GYMNASTICS

FRONT VAULT SKILLS

Level of Difficulty: A

Stacked panel mats (approximately 24″ high) are positioned perpendicular to the direction of motion.

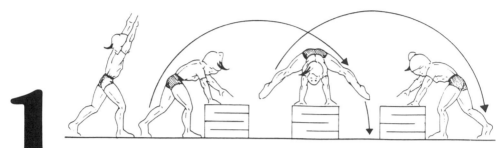

1 **1/2 Cartwheel Over** Move forward toward the mats, place both hands on top of the mats, and swing the back leg upward and to the side. Push off the front leg and continue the cartwheel motion, keeping the hips parallel to the mats, and land on the other side of the mats.

2 **3/4 Cartwheel Style Roundoff Over** Move forward toward the mats, place both hands on top of the mats, and swing the back leg upward and to the side. Push off the front leg and continue the cartwheel motion, raising the hips above horizontal, and turning 90 degrees while bringing the feet together to land facing the mats.

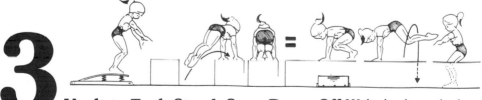

3 **Vault to Tuck Stand, Snap-Down Off** With the board placed close to the mats, bounce on the board, place the hands on the mat, jump off two feet turning 90 degrees, and land on top of the mats in a squat support. With support on the hands jump and snap the feet down while pushing off the hands to land standing beside the mat.

FRONT VAULT SKILLS

Level of Difficulty: B

Stacked panel mats (approximately 24" high) are positioned perpendicular to the direction of motion. A vaulting board is placed in front of the mats.

4 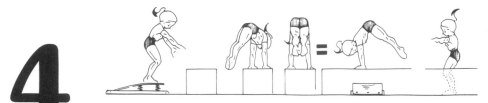 **Tucked Front Vault** Bounce on the board, vault upward, and over the mats, moving through a tuck support position on both hands. Land on both feet in a standing position beside the mat.

5 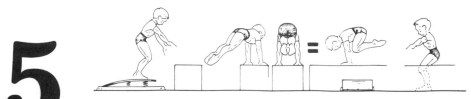 **Vault to Pike Support, Snap Down Off** Bounce on the board and with a two hand support vault upward bending at the hips to piked stand sideways on the mats. Extend the legs with support on the hands and snap down to a standing position beside the horse.

6 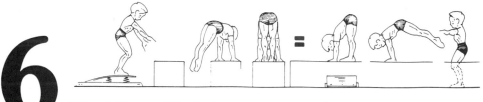 **Piked Front Vault** Bounce on the board, vault upward and over the mats, moving through a pike position on both hands. Land on both feet in a standing position beside the mat.

FRONT VAULT SKILLS

Level of Difficulty: C

Stacked panel mats (approximately 24" high) are positioned perpendicular to the direction of motion. A vaulting board is placed in front of the mats.

7 **Layout Front Vault** Bounce on the board and vault over the panel mats moving through a high stretched body position to land on both feet beside the mats.

8 **Front Vault, 90 Degree Turn** Bounce on the board and vault over the panel mats moving through a high stretched body position. Turn 90 degrees on the downward flight to land on both feet facing the mats.

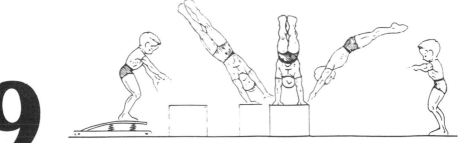

9 **3/4 Cartwheel with 90 Degree Turn** Run, hurdle, and rebound off the board to place the hands on the mats as the lower body rises and turns. Using a cartwheel motion, move through an inverted position, push off the mats, turn 90 degrees to land facing the mats. Show demi-plié before extending legs to stand.

> **What to Practice:**
> - When upside-down, be sure your head is in and eyes are focused on hands.
> - Keep legs extended, and maintain good straddle throughout.
> - Try to maintain control and balance from start to finish.

FLANK AND REAR VAULT SKILLS

Level of Difficulty: A

Stacked panel mats (approximately 24" high) are positioned perpendicular to the direction of motion.

1 **One Leg Hop Over (without board)** Walk up to mats, hop onto the mats with support of one hand and one foot (fingers of support hand pointing toward long end of the mats), then hop off on the other side of the mats to land standing beside the mats.

2 **One Leg Hop Over (with board)** Place a springboard in front of the mats. Bounce off two feet and jump to a one hand and one foot support on top of the mats. Push off the mats to a two foot landing, facing away from the mats.

3 **Modified Flank Vault** Place a springboard in front of the mats. Bounce off two feet to a two hand support position on top of the mats. Swing the legs to the side, bending the lower leg while lifting the arm on that side. Continue the motion over the mats, bring the feet together, and land facing away from the mats.

FLANK AND REAR VAULT SKILLS
Level of Difficulty: B

Stacked panel mats (approximately 24″ high) are positioned perpendicular to the direction of motion. A vaulting board is placed in front of the mats.

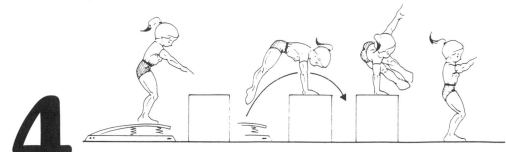

4 Piked Flank Vault Bounce off the board to a support on two hands. Swing both legs to one side, shifting body weight to the hand on the opposite side. Continue swinging the legs over the mat in a pike position to land facing away from the mats.

5 Stretched Flank Vault Perform this vault just as shown in the skill above, but with the body in a fully extended position.

6 Jump, 180 Degree Turn to Seat (without board) The springboard is removed. Place the hands on top of the mats and jump while pushing downward with the hands. Turn 180 degrees to a seated position on the mats.

FLANK AND REAR VAULT SKILLS

Level of Difficulty: C

Stacked panel mats (approximately 24″ high) are positioned perpendicular to the direction of motion. A vaulting board is placed in front of the mats.

7 **Bounce, 180 Degrees Turn to Seat (with board)** Bounce off the board to place the hands on top of the mats. Push downward with the hands and turn 180 degrees to a seated position on the mats.

8 **Vault to Piked Sit Position** Bounce off the board with the support of the hands on the mats. Lift the legs to the side while turning the body to a side seated position on top of the mats.

9 **Rear Vault** Run, hurdle, and rebound off the board. With support on the hands, lift both legs to the side, and pass over the mats in a pike position. Finish by landing beside the mats showing a demi-plié before extending to a stand.

What to Practice:

- Make sure that your initial support is on both hands.
- Support should be transferred from one hand to the other as the legs pass over the mats.
- Feet should be perpendicular to mats on landing.

I CAN DO GYMNASTICS

SQUAT VAULT SKILLS

Sequence A

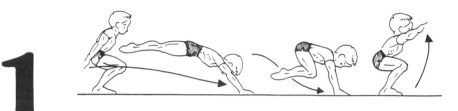

1 **Squat-Extend Jumps in a Series** From a squat position on the floor lean forward and push off the legs while reaching forward with the hands. With momentary support on the hands, bring the knees forward to return to a squat position. Repeat in a series of 3 to 5 jumps.

2 **Squat Thrusts** From a front leaning support on the floor, shift the weight to the hands and bring the knees forward to a squat position. Then return to a front leaning support and repeat the activity 3 to 5 times.

3 **Squat from Extended Body Position (feet elevated)** From a front leaning support with the feet and legs elevated on a folded panel mat, bring the knees forward to a squat position on the base mat with support on the hands. Extend to a stand.

SQUAT VAULT SKILLS

Sequence B

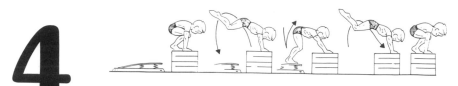

4 **Squat On, Bounce, Squat On** From a squat position on top of the mats, shift the weight onto the hands, extend the legs backward, and snap down to the board. Rebound off the board and return to a squat position on the mats.

5 **Squat On, Bounce, Squat On, Jump Off** Repeat skill 4 as shown above, but as the second squat position is achieved, immediately jump forward off the mats to land in a demi-plié. Extend to stand.

6 **Bounces to Squat On, Jump Off** From a stand on the springboard with hands on top of the mats, bounce 3 to 5 times and squat onto the mats. Immediately jump forward off the mats and land in demi-plié, raise to stand.

I CAN DO GYMNASTICS

SQUAT VAULT SKILLS

Sequence C

Stacked panel mats (approximately 24″ high) are positioned perpendicular to the direction of motion. A vaulting board is placed in front of the mats.

7 **Squat On, Jump Off (from walk)** Walk forward 3 to 5 steps, hurdle, and rebound off the board with two feet. Vault to a squat position on the mats, immediately jump forward off the mats and land in demi-plié , raise to a stand.

8 **Squat On, Jump Off (from run)** Repeat skill 7 as shown above, using 3 to 5 running steps.

9 **Squat Vault** Run 3 to 5 steps, hurdle, and rebound off the springboard with two feet. Reach forward with arms to a front support and at the same time push off the mat with both hands and tuck the knees. After passing over the mats, extend the legs to land in a demi-plié , rise to a stand.

Checklist for Vault Skills

Skill	Level of Difficulty			Date Skill Series Completed
	A	B	C	
Jump Series				
Front Vaults				
Flank and Rear Vaults				
Squat Vaults				

I CAN DO GYMNASTICS

4

On the Beam

The balance beam is a long narrow piece of wood or metal that is topped with a foam pad and tightly covered with material. The beam measures 4 inches wide by 16 feet long, and stands on an adjustable steel base.

The standard height of the balance beam for the Olympics and international competition is four feet (120 centimeters) from the floor. For younger and beginning gymnasts, the beam should be lowered. As an example, the acceptable height for the beam in the USGF Junior Olympic competitions is 45.25 inches for the junior division (ages 12-14) and 43.25 inches for the children's division (ages 9-11).

The beam you work on will have mats on both sides and at each end. The mats form "a gymnast safety zone". The beam you begin on may only be a few inches off the floor, but as you progress in gymnastics the beam will be higher. Falls are a little more dangerous from the beam, because of its height. It is important that you practice the safety landing skills from the beam, so that if you do fall you will do it the right way without having to think about it.

To be the best you can be on the balance beam requires a lot more than good balance, you must also constantly practice and develop your flexibility, grace, rhythm, tumbling ability, confidence, and concentration.

The progressions you will work through to learn beam skills are very important because they will help you to develop all of these skills correctly and safely.

The skills you will perform on the beam should be learned on the floor first, just like the tumbling skills in Chapter 2. It is a good idea to learn the skill on a floor mat and then practice it on a line on the floor before trying it on a low beam.

BALANCE BEAM SEQUENCES

Key to codes:

F   line on Floor

L   low beam

M   medium height beam (waist high)

H   high beam (47.25")

Bold type (**F, L, M, H**) indicates preferred height for the student to learn the skill or sequence.

Normal type (F, L, M, H) indicates other heights the at which the skill or sequence may be performed.

MOUNT SKILLS FOR THE BEAM

Level of Difficulty: A

1 **Step on to Balance Stand** Stand facing beam. Step up onto top of beam with one foot, bringing the other foot up to a balance stand on both feet. (**L**)

2 **Step on to Squat** Perform skill 1 as shown above, approaching from an oblique angle and lowering the body to a squat position, facing the end of the beam. (**L**)

What to Practice:
- Keep head and torso up, eyes focus to the end of the beam.
- Use the leg push to center your body on the beam.
- Maintain control and balance when lowering to the squat position.

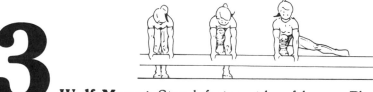

3 **Wolf Mount** Stand facing side of beam. Place hands on top of beam and jump up, bringing one leg up on top of beam to place foot on beam between hands. Then bring the other leg up to place it on top of the beam, outside of the hands, extended toward the end of the beam. (**L, M**)

MOUNT SKILLS FOR THE BEAM

Level of Difficulty: B

4 **Front Support Mount** Stand facing side of beam. Place hands on top of beam and push off floor (or board) to place the front of your thighs against the beam, supporting the body weight with extended arms. (**M**, H)

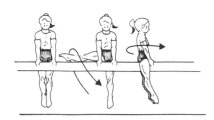

5 **Front Support to Straddle Sit** From front leaning support position, swing one leg up and over the side of the beam, turning the body to the side to a straddle sit position on the top of the beam, hands on beam in front of body facing the end of the beam. (If necessary, keep one foot on the floor for balance.) (**M**, H)

6 **Jump to One-Foot Squat Support** Stand facing side of beam. Place hands on top of beam and jump off floor (or board) to place one foot on top of beam between hands, leaving the other leg extended beside the beam. (**M**, H)

MOUNT SKILLS FOR THE BEAM

Level of Difficulty: C

7 **Step to Side Sit, Leg Over** Step toward beam, pushing off floor (or board) and sit sideways on the beam, weight on one hip with inside leg bent and outside leg extended (stag sit or cross riding seat.) Lift inside leg up and over beam to a straddle sit. (**M**, H)

8 **Step to Side Sit, Both Legs Over** Step toward beam pushing off floor (or board) and sit sideways on beam. Swing inside leg up and over as shown above, then lift other leg up and over the beam to cross riding seat position on the opposite side of the beam from the start position.(**M**, H)

What to Practice:
- Use your arms for balance and support on the beam.
- Lift legs slowly and with control
- Keep head and torso up, eyes focused on end of the beam.

9 **Scissor Mount** Start diagonally from one side of the beam. Place the inside hand on the top of the beam and step off the opposite leg. Lift the leg next to the beam up and over the beam, immediately followed by the push off leg. Land in a side sitting position on the beam with one hand on the beam behind the body (legs on the opposite side from the starting position.) (**M**, H)

LOCOMOTOR ACTIVITIES FOR THE BEAM

Level of Difficulty: A

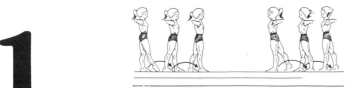

1 **Walk Forward/Backward** Walk forward and backward by placing one foot in front or behind the other. (**F, L,** M, H)

2 **Dip Steps Forward and Backward** Walk forward by bending one knee and "dipping" the other foot down the side of the beam, then bringing it up to place it on top of the beam in front of the support foot (reverse the process when walking backward.) (**L**, M, H)

What to Practice:
- Keep your head up, eyes focused toward the end of the beam.
- Maintain balance and control throughout.
- The knee bend and leg swing should be done with a rhythmic movement.

3 **Slide Steps to the Side** Facing the side of the beam, slide one foot to the side and close the other foot to it (move right, then left). (**F, L,** M, H)

LOCOMOTOR ACTIVITIES FOR THE BEAM

Level of Difficulty: B

4 **Lift Steps Forward and Backward** Stand facing the end of the beam. Walk forward by extending one leg up in front of the body and placing it back on the beam in front of the first foot. Continue down the beam in the same manner. (To perform backwards, lift leg up behind the body.) (**F, L,** M, H)

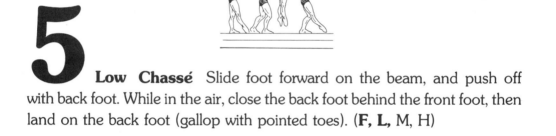

5 **Low Chassé** Slide foot forward on the beam, and push off with back foot. While in the air, close the back foot behind the front foot, then land on the back foot (gallop with pointed toes). (**F, L,** M, H)

6 **Step Hops** Step forward on one foot, and hop on that foot, bringing the other foot up in the air. Then step forward and hop on the opposite foot, lifting the free foot into the air. (**F, L,** M, H)

LOCOMOTOR ACTIVITIES FOR THE BEAM

Level of Difficulty: C

7 Low Stretch Jump Stand with one foot in front of the other foot. Push off both feet to perform a low stretch jump and land on both feet on the beam in the SLP. (**F, L,** M, H)

8 Low Stride Leap Push off the beam from one foot to land forward on the beam on the other foot, in the SLP. (**F, L,** M, H)

What to Practice:
- Make sure your take-off push with your leg is strong.
- Opposite arm is in-front of you when you jump.
- The demi-plié in when you land in the SLP is most important.

9 Low Tuck/Squat Jump Push off from both feet to perform a low tuck jump on the beam, landing on both feet on the beam in the SLP. Do not grasp legs. (**F, L,** M, H)

STATIC BALANCE SKILLS ON THE BEAM
Level of Difficulty: A

1 **Lunge** Place one foot in front of the other foot and bend the knee of the front leg, extending the rear leg, body upright and weight over both legs. (**F, L,** M, H)

2 **Front Leaning Support** From a stand, squat down to place hands in front of the feet on the beam. Extend legs backward along the beam, keeping the legs and arms extended. Keep weight over the feet and arms. (**F, L,** M, H)

3 **Kneeling Pose** From the extended position as shown above in skill 2, bend one knee and place it on the beam. Turn back leg so foot is on its side on the beam. Keep hands on beam to balance then lift hands from beam to an upright balance position. (**F, L,** M, H)

STATIC BALANCE SKILLS ON THE BEAM
Level of Difficulty: B

4 **Shin Scale, Straddle to V-Sit** From kneeling pose, place hands on top of the beam in front of the knee and raise and extend the back leg up from the beam, with arms extended. Lower the extended leg and bent leg to come to a straddle sitting position on the beam. Then place the hands on the beam behind the hips and extend the legs in the air in front of the body into a V position.(F, L, **M**, H)

5 **Low Arabesque** Stand on one foot with trunk erect. Lift other foot and leg backward and upward, extending the leg off the beam with the knee facing the side or down. (**F, L,** M, H)

> ### What to Practice:
> - Keep support leg in demi-plié
> - Arms should be extended to the sides.
> - Back leg must be straight.
> - Maintain balance and control throughout the skill.

6 **Pique Balance (1-leg balance, foot at ankle)** Stand on beam and lift one foot up to touch the ankle of the support leg by bending at the knee of the working leg. Hold this position. (**F, L,** M, H)

STATIC BALANCE SKILLS ON THE BEAM
Level of Difficulty: C

7 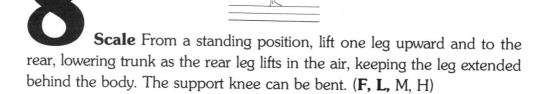 **Passé Balance (1-leg balance, foot at knee)** Stand on beam and raise one foot up to touch the knee of the support leg by bending at the knee of the working leg. (**F, L,** M, H)

8 **Scale** From a standing position, lift one leg upward and to the rear, lowering trunk as the rear leg lifts in the air, keeping the leg extended behind the body. The support knee can be bent. (**F, L,** M, H)

9 **Y-Scale** From standing position, slowly and with control lift one leg to the side. Extend and hold the leg with your hand, either above or below the knee. (**F, L,** M, H)

I CAN DO GYMNASTICS

NON-LOCOMOTOR ACTIVITIES ON THE BEAM

Level of Difficulty: A

1 **Lunge, 90 Degree Turn to Straddle Stand** Stand in a lunge position facing the end of the beam. Turn 90 degrees to the side to end in a straddle stand position facing out. (**F, L,** M, H)

2 **180 Degree Turn** Stand facing the end of the beam with one foot in front of the other. Rise up on the balls of the feet and turn 180 degrees toward the back to face the other end of the beam (pivot turn.) (**F, L,** M, H)

3 **Squat Turn** Stand facing the end of the beam. Lower to a squat position and turn 180 degrees toward the back foot to face the other end of the beam, in the squat position. (**F, L,** M, H)

NON-LOCOMOTOR ACTIVITIES FOR THE BEAM

Level of Difficulty: B

4 Arabesque Turn (180 Degrees) Stand facing the end of the beam. Raise the back leg to low arabesque position. Rise up on the ball of the foot and perform a 180 degree turn (pivot turn) to face the opposite end of the beam, with the arabesque leg finishing in front. (**F, L,** M, H)

What to Practice:
- Maintain control in the arabesque.
- Arms should swing up and then lower to your sides with the turn.
- Keep hips and shoulders in alignment throughout the skill.

5 Forward Swing Turn Lift one leg up in front and perform a 180 degree turn on the other foot to finish with the leg up in back of the body, then lower the body to a lunge position.(**F, L,** M, H)

6 Backward Swing Turn Swing one leg up in front, then down and through to the back while performing a 180 degree turn toward the swinging leg on the support leg to finish with the swinging leg in front. Lower to a lunge position. (**F, L,** M, H)

NON-LOCOMOTOR ACTIVITIES FOR THE BEAM

Level of Difficulty: C

7  **Lunge Series** Stand in a lunge position. Lower to low lunge, then place hands on the beam in front of the bent leg. Lower to a shin scale, then to the straddle sit position. (**F, L,** M, H)

8  **Stand Series** Begin in a straddle sit position on the beam facing the end of the beam. Swing legs behind body and place feet on top of the beam. Push up and back by extending your arms to come to a squat stand position, then to a stretched stand. (**F, L,** M, H)

9 **Body Wave** Move body segments in succession from bottom up and top down. (**F, L,** M, H)

What to Practice:
- Move body segments rhythmically.
- There should be a smooth transition from contraction to extension.
- Maintain balance and control throughout.

TUMBLING SKILLS FOR THE BEAM

Level of Difficulty: A

  **Beam Walking on All Fours** Walk across beam with hands and feet on the beam, body will move from tuck to piked position. (**F, L,** M, H)

 **Squat to Pike** From standing position, squat down and place hands on beam in front of feet, then extend legs into pike position. Return to squat position, then extend to stand. (**F, L,** M, H)

 **Hop Across Beam with Hand Support** Squat down and place hands on beam in front of feet. Raise one leg, extending it behind the body. Move hands forward and hop forward on the support foot. (**F, L**, M, H)

I CAN DO GYMNASTICS

TUMBLING SKILLS FOR THE BEAM

Level of Difficulty: B

4 **Single Leg Low Swing Up** Squat down and place hands on beam in front of feet. Rise to a pike position. Lift one leg up and back (low) and bring it down to beam. Support leg will come slightly off beam (use mats stacked up to level of top beam). (**F, L,** M, H)

5 **3/4 Handstand Switch Legs** From standing position, lean forward and place hands on beam. As one leg swings up in the air, the other leg will come slightly off of the beam. Switch legs and land on the opposite foot. (**F, L,** M, H)

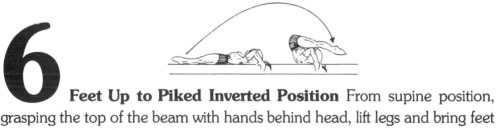

6 **Feet Up to Piked Inverted Position** From supine position, grasping the top of the beam with hands behind head, lift legs and bring feet over head to touch toes to beam, or bring feet as close to the beam as possible. (**F, L,** M, H)

TUMBLING SKILLS FOR THE BEAM

Level of Difficulty: C

7

Roll Back and Return to Sit From tuck sitting position on beam, roll back to touch feet over head on beam, then return to tuck sitting position. (**F, L**, M, H)

8

Straddle Forward Roll Over (low beam) From a straddle position over the low beam (feet are on the floor), place hands on the beam, lower upper back to beam behind hands, roll forward coming up to a straddle stand position (same as starting position). (**L**)

What to Practice:
- Make sure your hands support your weight as the roll begins.
- Roll straight down the beam.
- Roll slowly and with control.

9

Back Roll Start from tuck/pike sitting position on the beam. Roll back and simultaneously bend at the hips to bring feet up and over head. Push with hands and toes (behind head) on beam, roll over to finish on hands and shins. (**L**, M, H)

BEAM DISMOUNT SKILLS

Level of Difficulty: A

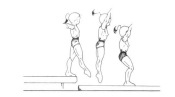

1 **Step Off End** From standing position on the beam, step off beam to two foot landing on mat in the SLP. Rise to a stand. (**L**)

2 **Stretch Jump Dismount** From a standing position on the beam, jump upward and forward to a stretched position off the end/side to a mat with a two foot landing in the SLP. Rise to a stand. (**L,** M, H)

What to Practice:
- Use your arm swing to assist your jump.
- Keep torso upright, eyes focused toward end of mat.
- Maintain balance and control in the SLP.

3 **Tuck Jump Dismount** From a standing on beam, jump to a tuck position in the air from end or side of the beam, land on mat on both feet in the SLP. Rise to a stand. (**L,** M, H)

BEAM DISMOUNT SKILLS

Level of Difficulty: B

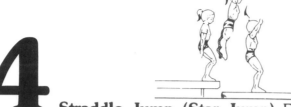

4 **Straddle Jump (Star Jump)** From a standing position on the beam, push off to a jump in the air, straddling legs to the side. Bring legs back together in the air to land on the mat on both feet in the SLP. Rise to a stand. (**L, M, H**)

5 **Stretched Jump With 180 Degree Twist to Land** From starting position, jump off the beam, performing a 180 degree twist to land facing the beam on the mat on both feet in the SLP. Rise to a stand. (**L**, M, H)

What to Practice:
- Arms should be lifted to extended overhead position.
- Keep body vertical and stretched.
- Maintain balance and control in the SLP.

6 **Jump off with Twists** Stand on the beam, facing the end. Jump off beam to perform 90 degree twist. Land on mat on both feet. Jump and twist 180 degrees, land and come to a momentary pause. (**L**)

BEAM DISMOUNT SKILLS

Level of Difficulty: C

7 **Jump Off with 180 Degrees Twist, Land 180 Degrees Twist** Stand on beam, facing end/side. Jump from beam to perform a 180 degree twist, land on the mat on both feet in demi-plié . Immediately jump with 180 degree twist, land on two feet in SLP. Rise to a stand. (**L,** M)

8 **Front Support to Front Dismount** From a front leaning support position on the beam, bend the knees and push upward off the beam, lowering the legs and landing on both feet in SLP. Rise to a stand. (**L,** M, H)

9 **3/4 Handstand Switch Leg Dismount** From standing position on the beam, place hands on beam to lift legs up into the air, switching legs. Push slightly to the side with the arms to bring both legs together to the mat, coming to a momentary pause. (**L,** M, H)

Balance Beam Skill Checklist

Skill	Level of Difficulty			Date Skill Series Completed
	A	B	C	
Mounts				
Locomotor Activities				
Static Balance				
Non-Locomotor Activities				
Tumbling				
Dismounts				

I CAN DO GYMNASTICS

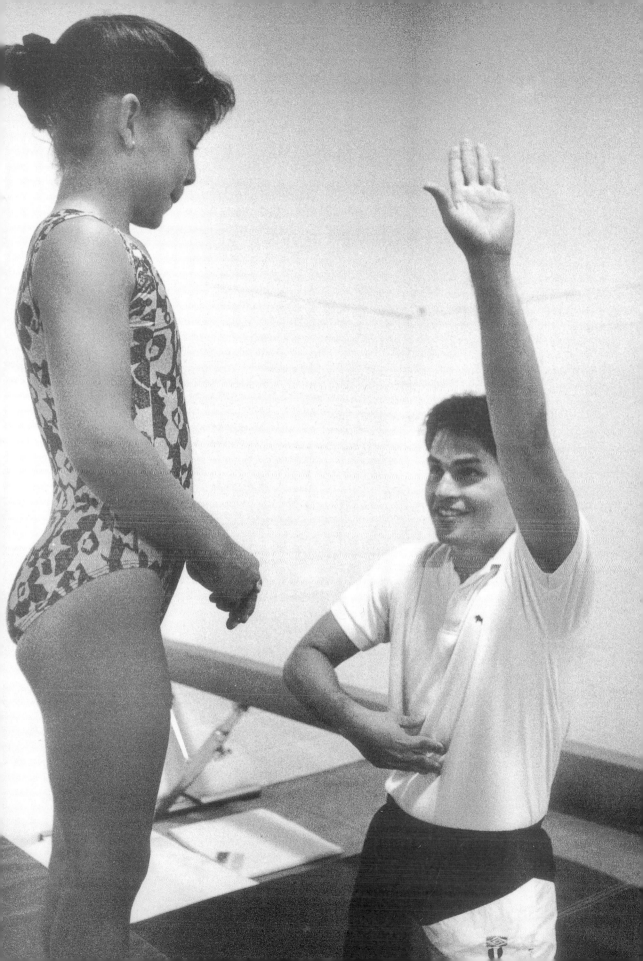

5

Around the Bar

The bars are very different events for men and women. Women use the uneven bars to demonstrate their more graceful skills, while men must demonstrate more strength in their routines on both the horizontal bar and the parallel bars. While the equipment and the routines are different for men and women, the basic skills remain the same.

Bar skills are difficult to learn because they require a great deal of upper body strength. Developing your strength may take a long time, but as you progress through these exercises you will find yourself growing stronger and developing the technique you will need to progress to the more complicated moves.

BACKWARD CIRCLING SKILLS FOR THE SINGLE BAR

Level of Difficulty: A

Note: Bar should be adjusted to your chest height.

1 **Waist to Bar** From a stand, step forward and lift one leg upward, pulling the body (waist) to the bar and slowly return to the floor.

2 **Stretch Hip Pullover** From a stand with hands in an overgrip, step up to a folded mat placed slightly in front of the bar, push off the mat with one leg while lifting the other leg over the bar. Pull bar toward the waist, rotating the shoulders backward over the bar. Finish in a front support.

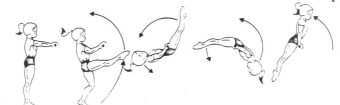

3 **Back Hip Pullover** From a stand, with hands in overgrip, push off the floor with one leg while lifting the other leg over the bar. Pull bar toward the waist, rotating the shoulders backward over the bar. Finish in a front support.

What to Practice:

- Keep your arms bent as your feet leave the floor
- Bar contact should be at your waist
- Remember to shift hands around the bar to support your position

---

I CAN DO GYMNASTICS

BACKWARD CIRCLING SKILLS FOR
THE SINGLE BAR

Level of Difficulty: B

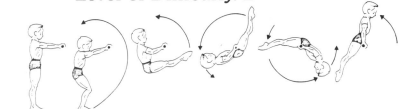

4 **Back Hip Pullover** From a stand, overgrip the bar, jump from both feet pulling the bar to the waist. Rotate backward over the bar.

5 **Cast** From a front support, bend at the waist with the shoulders forward, thrust legs backward and upward (hip extension) to horizontal to rise off the bar, return to the bar before again bending at the waist.

> **What to Practice:**
> - Your shoulders should move forward as your body pikes
> - Keep shoulders forward as your legs extend behind you
> - Maintain control when lowering to support

6 **Cast, Back Hip Circle (shown with spot)** From a front support, cast, then rock backward, creating enough momentum to pull the bar toward the waist to rotate backward around the bar.

BACKWARD CIRCLING SKILLS ON A SINGLE BAR

Level of Difficulty: C

7 Cast to Back Hip Circle From a front support, cast away from the bar. When contacting the bar, shift backward bending at the waist, arms and legs slightly bent to make the body smaller for rotation backward around the bar.

8 Back Hip Circle (straight/piked) From a front support, cast away from the bar. When contacting the bar, shift backward bending at the waist and keeping the legs extended while rotating backward around the bar.

9 Back Hip Circle (straight/straight) From a front support position, cast away from the bar. When you contact the bar with your extended arms and body, lean back to rotate backward around the bar.

CIRCLING FORWARD SKILLS ON A SINGLE BAR

Level of Difficulty: A

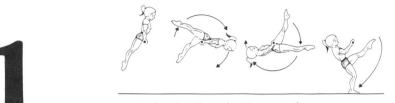

1 **Forward Roll (split legs)** From a front support with overgrip, roll over the bar forward (split legs) and slowly lower body to the mat.

2 **Forward Roll (undergrip or mixed grip)** From a front support with the under/mixed grip, roll over bar forward (split legs) and slowly lower your body to the mat.

3 **Jump to Roll Over (undergrip)** From a stand, grip the bar with an undergrip, jump to support with undergrip (bar no more than chest high), roll over the bar with split leg position and slowly lower to a stand.

What to Practice:

- Make sure wrists shift to achieve support
- Maintain control while in the support position
- Roll forward should be SLOW
- Keep grip on the bar until full support on the legs is achieved

---

CIRCLING FORWARD ON A SINGLE BAR

Level of Difficulty: B

4 **Forward Roll Over to Single Knee Hang** From a front support, single leg cut, then change to under or mixed grip, roll over the bar forward to a single knee hang.

5 **Single Knee Up** From a single knee hang, extend the non-hang leg out, down, and back generating force to rotate around the bar forward to finish in a stride support.

What to Practice:

- Leg extension will generate pendular body swing
- Arms should pull at the peak of the backward swing
- Shift wrists to achieve support position

6 **Rock Back to Single Knee Up** From a front support, single leg cut to single leg support, rock back to single knee hang, extend the non-hang leg out, down, and back generating force to rotate around the bar to finish in a stride support.

CIRCLING FORWARD ON A SINGLE BAR

Level of Difficulty: C

7 **Single Knee Forward Roll Over** From a front support, single leg cut to support, change to undergrip to roll over the bar forward to a single knee hang. A spot may be necessary.

8 **1/2 Circle Forward** Perform skill 7 as shown above with both legs extended, finish in an inverted stride hang.

What to Practice:
- Hands must begin in undergrip
- Lower yourself slowly and with control
- Hands should maintain grip on the bar until feet gain support on the floor

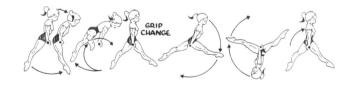

9 **Stride Circle** From a front support, single leg cut to support, change to undergrip, extend the cut leg forward placing the back leg against the bar and shifting foward, circle the bar forward in a stride position to finish in a stride support. (A spot may be necessary.)

CASTING TO A SOLE CIRCLE ON A SINGLE BAR

Level of Difficulty: A

1 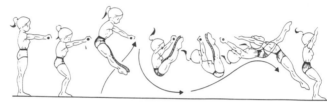 **Jump Underswing, Shoot to a Stand** From a stand with extended arms and overgrip, jump and bend at the waist, bringing ankles close to the bar. Hold this position and swing under the bar extending the body upward and outward. Release hands and land on the mat in the SLP. Return to a stand.

2 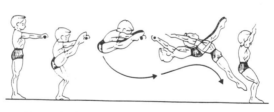 **Jump Straddled Underswing** From a stand with extended arms and overgrip, jump while bending at the waist to straddle legs with feet close to the bar. Hold this position and swing under the bar, releasing hands to land on the mat in the SLP. Return to a stand.

3 **Climb to a Straddle Underswing** From a stand with extended arms and overgrip, lift one leg (bar no more than chest high) placing that foot on the bar outside hand position. Jump off other leg, lifting it, to flex at the waist. Place the other foot outside other hand (hold the position). At the end of the underswing, release the bar to land on mat in SLP. Return to a stand.

> **What to Practice:**
> - Your feet should be placed directly beside your hands
> - Arms should remain straight during jump from the supporting leg
> - Feet should touch the bar until the peak of your upswing
> - ALWAYS show proper landing technique

CASTING TO A SOLE CIRCLE ON A SINGLE BAR
Level of Difficulty: B

4 Jump to Straddle Sole Circle Dismount From a stand with extended arms and overgrip, jump to a straddled position bending at the waist, placing the feet on the bar outside of the hands (hold position). At the end of the underswing, release the bar to land on the mat in SLP. Return to a stand.

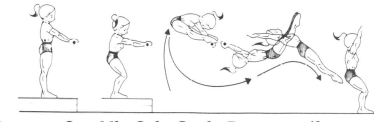

5 Jump to Straddle Sole Circle Dismount (from stacked mats) From a standing position on folded panel mats with extended arms and overgrip, jump to a straddle position bending at the waist. Place feet on the bar outside the hands (hold position). At the end of the underswing, release the bar to land on the mat in SLP. Return to a stand.

6 Jump Off Forward (shown with a spot) From a front support position, bring one foot up on the bar, slide foot close to the hands, move hands so foot is between hands (spotter will hold your shoulder and your wrist). Push to a stand on both feet, then jump forward off bar to land on the mat in SLP. Return to a stand.

CASTING TO A SOLE CIRCLE ON A SINGLE BAR

Level of Difficulty: C

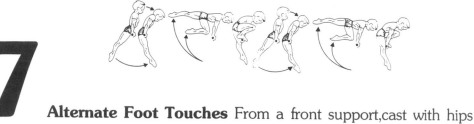

7 **Alternate Foot Touches** From a front support, cast with hips shoulder height, place one foot on the bar outside hands, return to a support. Repeat alternating feet. (This may be spotted.)

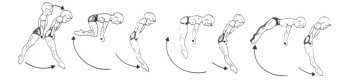

8 **Casts in Tuck, Pike, and Straddle** From a front support, cast hips shoulder height and tuck, return to the bar. Recast showing pike, return to bar. Recast showing straddle, return to bar.

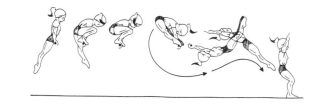

9 **Climb to Straddle Sole Circle Dismount** From a front support, climb to a straddle stand on the bar, lean back (a spot may be needed), underswing, release the bar to land on the mat in SLP. Return to a stand.

SWINGS AND TURNS TO SWING ON A SINGLE BAR

Level of Difficulty: A

1  **Run Under, 180 Degree Turn, Run Through** From a stand with extended arms and overgrip, run under the bar, stop and release the bar, 180 degree turn, regrip with overgrip and run through again.

2  **Run Under, 180 Degree Turn, Tuck Swing** From a stand position with arms extended and hands in overgrip, swing under the bar, stop and release bar, 180 degree turn, regrip with overgrip, swing under in a tuck position.

3 **Tuck Swing, 180 Degree, Tuck Swing** From a stand position with arms extended and overgrip, swing under the bar in a tuck position, stop and release bar, 180 degree turn, regrip in overgrip and swing under the bar in the tuck position, stop.

SWINGS AND TURNS TO SWING ON SINGLE BAR

Level of Difficulty: B

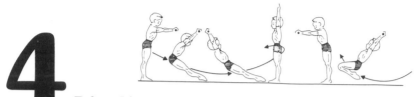

4 **Pike Glide, 180 Degree Turn, Tuck Swing** From a stand with extended arms and overgrip, swing under the bar in a pike position, stop and release the bar, 180 degree turn, regrip in overgrip and swing under the bar in piked position.

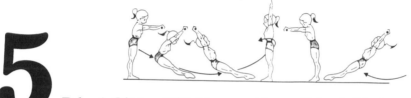

5 **Piked Glide, 180 Degree Turn, Piked Glide** From a stand with extended arms and overgrip, swing under the bar in a pike position, stop and release the bar, 180 degree turn, regrip in overgrip and swing under the bar in piked position.

6 **Tuck Swing, 180 Degree Turn, Tuck Swing (mixed grip)** From a stand with extended arms and mixed grip, swing under bar in a tuck position, stop and release one hand, 180 degree turn regrip with mixed grip, swing under the bar in tuck position.

What to Practice:
- Undergrip hands should shift during the swing through
- Grip should release after leg support
- Maintain shoulder and hip alignment during swing

SWING AND TURNS TO SWING ON THE SINGLE BAR

Level of Difficulty: C

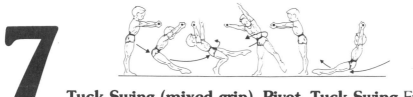

7 **Tuck Swing (mixed grip), Pivot, Tuck Swing** From a stand with extended arms and mixed grip, swing under the bar in a tuck position, stop and release the undergrip hand, pivot on the overgrip hand, regrasp in mixed grip and swing under the bar in tuck position.

8 **Tuck Swing, 180 Degree Turn, Glide Tap to 1-Leg Hang** From a stand with extended arms and overgrip, swing under the bar in tuck position with a 180 degree turn to stand, hesitate and regrip in overgrip, swing under the bar in pike position. At extension of the swing, tap feet on the mat to bring one leg up between hands to a single knee hang.

9 **Tuck Swing, 180 Degree Turn, Pike Glide Tap to Single Knee Up** From a stand with extended arms and overgrip, swing under the bar in tuck position with a 180 degree turn to a stand, hesitate and regrip in overgrip, swing under the bar in a pike. At extension of the swing, tap feet on the mat to bring one leg up between hands and swing again to a single knee-up to a stride support.

SUPPORTS AND TURNS TO SWING ON THE SINGLE BAR

Level of Difficulty: A

1 **Single Leg Cut, 180 Degree Turn** From a front support with overgrip, single leg cut (L), change right hand to undergrip, turn right reaching the left hand across chest to regrasp the bar. During the turn, bring right leg back over to finish in front support. (This sequence may be reversed.)

2 **Front Support, Single Leg Over** From a front support with mixed grip, single leg cut to overgrip side, pivot to undergrip side to front support. Regrip and swing front leg back to finish in front support.

What to Practice:

- Keep arms straight in support
- Weight should shift to support arm during leg cuts
- Show support in stride position and final front support

3 **Single Leg Cut, 180 Degree Turn, Underswing Dismount** Repeat skill 1 as shown above to rock back to underswing dismount to land on the mat in SLP.

SUPPORTS AND TURNS TO SWING ON THE SINGLE BAR

Level of Difficulty: B

4 **Single Leg Cut, Turn** From front support, single leg cut (L), sit onthe bar, take left hand, place it inside the right hand in overgrip position, take right hand to reach behind and regrip the bar. Lift the body and turn, sitting on right hip. (This sequence may be reversed.)

5 **Single Leg Cut, Turn, Single Leg Cut Back** Repeat skill 4 as shown above with a single leg cut back.

6 **Single Leg Cut, Turn, Rock Back to Knee Swing** Repeat skill 4 as shown above, rock back to single knee hang, swing back to single knee up to finish in stride support.

SUPPORTS AND TURNS TO SWING ON THE SINGLE BAR

Level of Difficulty: C

7 **Single Leg Cut, Other Leg Over, 180 Degree Turn** From a front support, single leg cut. Bring the other leg over to rear seat position. Change one hand to undergrip. Release other hand and reach across chest to regrasp bar while executing 180 degree turn to finish in a front support.

8 **Single Leg Cut, Other Leg Over, 180 Degree Turn, Underswing Dismount** Repeat skill 7 as shown above, as front support position is attained, shift backward and execute underswing dismount to land on mat in SLP. Finish in a stand.

9 **Single Leg Cuts Left-Right-Return, Underswing Dismount** From a front support, single leg cut one leg, then other leg to rear support. Execute single leg cuts back to front support. Immediate underswing dismount to land on the mat in SLP. Finish in a stand.

What to Practice:

- Maintain control and balance while executing leg cuts.
- Arms should remain straight in support
- ALWAYS demonstrate proper landing technique

Single Bar Skill Checklist

Skill	Level of Difficulty			Date Skill Series Completed
	A	B	C	
Circling Backward				
Circling Forward				
Casting to Sole Circle				
Swing and Turns to Swing				
Supports and Turns to Swing				

6

Rhythmic Gymnastics Skills

If you like music and dance and enjoy being creative, you will really enjoy rhythmic gymnastics. Rhythmic gymnastics is a combination of gymnastics skills and dance. It is one of the most beautiful and graceful of all sports events. It is also different from the other gymnastics skills in this book because the gymnasts do not work on fixed equipment. Rhythmic gymnasts perform their skills using light handheld apparatus including rope, hoop, ball, and ribbon.

The size of the rhythmic floor is the same as that in artistic gymnastics. However, only a carpet is required since the gymnasts don't perform tumbling skills. High-level rhythmic gymnasts need to perform in a room with a very high ceiling (30 to 40 feet high) because they throw the apparatus so high.

The great part about rhythmic skills is that once you have a grasp of the fundamentals, there are no limits on what you can do. There is room for endless creativity in movement, and best of all, these skills can be practiced with some equipment you may already have at home: ribbons, balls, jump ropes, and hoops.

ROPE - CIRCLING SKILLS

1 **Overhead** A double rope held in one hand is circled in a horizontal plan above the head. Use each hand, and perform the circle in both directions.

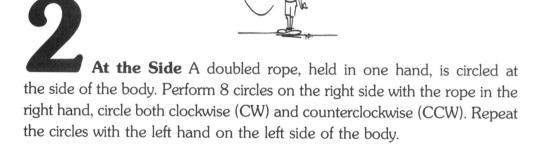

2 **At the Side** A doubled rope, held in one hand, is circled at the side of the body. Perform 8 circles on the right side with the rope in the right hand, circle both clockwise (CW) and counterclockwise (CCW). Repeat the circles with the left hand on the left side of the body.

3 **In Front** A doubled rope, held in one hand, is circled in a horizontal plane in front of the body. Use each hand and in both directions as described above.

4 **Figure Eight** A "Figure Eight" is achieved by holding a doubled rope in one hand and executing a circle, counterclockwise (CCW), on the right side of the body, then a clockwise (CW) circle on the left side of the body. Repeat the entire motion eight times.

ROPE - SWINGING

1 **Side to Side** Hold the rope by the ends, one in each hand, and swing the rope side to side in front of the body.

2 **Front to Back** Hold the rope by the ends, one in each hand, and swing the rope forward then backward on the right side of the body. Repeat the activity on the left side of the body.

ROPE - JUMPING AND HOPPING

1 **Jump on a Spot** Jump on a spot without a rope by lifting the knees with the arms relaxed by the sides and rotate the hands as if turning an imaginary rope. Jump 16 times. Repeat the activity using a rope without missing a jump.

What to Practice:
Without rope:

- Relax your shoulders
- Keep eyes and head up
- Arms should be relaxed by your side

With rope:

- All of the above
- Keep jumping continuous

2 **Hop, then Jump** Four hops are performed on each leg, followed by eight jumps on a spot from two feet.

What to Practice:
On one foot:

- Maintain free leg in a controlled position
- Keep body upright
- Arms and shoulders should be relaxed
- Eyes and head up

On two feet:

- Maintain extended body line

3 **Traveling Hops and Pose** Eight traveling, hopping steps forward are performed followed by an optional balance on one foot, incorporating the use of the rope. The performer returns with another eight hopping steps and performs a balance with the rope on the knees.

What to Practice:
- Hopping should be continuous
- Relax shoulders and arms
- Keep eyes and head up
- Hold balance for two seconds

4 **Side to Side Jump** Jumping from a two foot take-off is executed with a side-to-side jump each time.

5  **Cross Over** While jumping from two feet the arms are crossed in front of the body on the downward swing of the rope. The arms are uncrossed on the next turn of the rope and the rope is jumped over again.

6  **Group Activities With a Long Rope** The rope is swung from side to side. Players, in turn, jump over the rope eight times. The person in the middle jumps the turning rope eight times.

7  **Double Turns** Rebounding from two feet the performer executes a double turn of the rope.

ROPE - THROWING AND CATCHING

 Swing Out and Back Holding one end of the rope which trails behind the body, the rope is swung upward and forward into the air. As it turns back on itself the performer catches the returning free end with the other hand.

What to Practice:

- Keep "wrinkles" out of the rope.
- Catch at the end of the rope should be clean.
- Maintain controlled posture throughout.

Circle, Toss, and Catch Circling the doubled rope clockwise (CW), both ends held in one hand, lift the arm (from the shoulder), releasing the rope at the top of the reach. Catch the rope as it falls, by the ends, one in each hand.

SUPPLEMENTAL ROPE ACTIVITIES

Balances and Poses Support on: feet, foot, knee(s), back, bottom, side, shoulders. Demonstrate various balances.

Around an arm   **Around the body**

Body Wrap Be sure to practice with plenty of space.

HOOP - ROLLING

1 **Side to Side** Holding the hoop with both hands on the top, use both hands to roll the hoop from side to side.

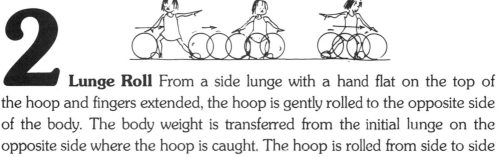

2 **Lunge Roll** From a side lunge with a hand flat on the top of the hoop and fingers extended, the hoop is gently rolled to the opposite side of the body. The body weight is transferred from the initial lunge on the opposite side where the hoop is caught. The hoop is rolled from side to side a total of four times.

What to Practice:

- Keep arm extended
- Hoop should roll in one plane
- Make transition from side to side smooth and rhythmical

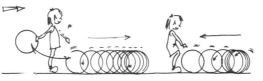

3 **Back Spinning** With a sweeping action from behind the body, the hoop is swung forward and given a backward "flick" just at the point of release. The hoop will roll forward and then return in "boomerang" fashion. (Called back spinning.)

What to Practice:

- Keep swinging action smooth
- Arm should follow through after releasing hoop
- Roll hoop in vertical plane

4 **Roll and Jump Over** From a small swing at the side of the body, roll the hoop forward. Then, run two or three steps and jump over the hoop. A small hoop should be used for this activity.

5 **Backspin, Kick, and Catch** From a small swing at the side of the body, backspin the hoop, as the hoop returns, kick it vertically and catch it on its downward path.

HOOP - SPINNING

1 **Spin in Place** Holding the hoop with both hands on top, spin the hoop in place by turning first one hand, then the other, slowly, without letting go.

2 **Spin and Kick** Place the hoop on the ground holding it with one hand. Spin the hoop about its vertical axis and swing one leg over it. Repeat the activity with the opposite leg.

3 **Spin in Both Hands** The hoop is spun between outstretched arms for the count of eight.

What to Practice:
- Keep axis of spin horizontal
- Maintain control of standing posture throughout
- Keep head upright

4 **Spin and Run, Skip, or Jump** The hoop is spun on the ground about its vertical axis. Various activities can be performed while the hoop is spinning: Run around the hoop, skip around the hoop, jump over the hoop.

HOOP - CIRCLING

1 **Circle on Both Arms** The hoop is held in a front position, resting on both wrists. Rotation is achieved by circling both arms together.

2 **Circle on One Hand** The hoop is held in one hand in a side position away from the body. Rotation is achieved by rotating the wrist with the fingers closed and thumb up.

3 **Circle on One Hand and Walk** Holding the hoop on one hand, in the side position, initiate rotation. The rotations are performed for the count of eight and then stopped and repeated for eight forward walking steps.

What to Practice:
- Make sure rotating hoop remains in one plane
- Maintain upright posture
- Keep your sight straight ahead

HOOP - THROWING AND CATCHING

1 **Swing From One Hand to the Other** The hoop is gripped in one hand and swung forward, backward, and forward; taken in the other hand, and swung backward, forward, and backward.

What to Practice:
- Keep swinging hoop in a vertical plane
- Your torso should stay upright
- Arms should stay straight, but you may need to bend at the bottom of the swing

2 **Swing, Toss, and Catch** The hoop is swung down and backward by the side with simultaneous knee bends, then forward and upward, released, and subsequently caught. The activity is performed four times on each side.

Additional Throwing and Catching Activities
- Catch while standing, balancing, or kneeling
- Catch after traveling or springing activity
- Catch while traveling, leaping, or jumping

SUPPLEMENTAL HOOP ACTIVITIES

1 **Step In and Out (Side to Side)** The hoop is held vertically to the side. The arm slowly sweeps down, the hoop is tilted towards a horizontal plane and two quick steps into the hoop are executed. This is followed by two quick steps in the reverse direction out of the hoop and the whole process is repeated holding the hoop with the other arm.

2 **Step In and Out (Forward and Back)** Using the preferred hand the performer repeats the above activity walking forward and stepping in and out of the hoop while moving forward (in) and backward (out).

What to Practice:

- Sweeping action of the hoop should be continuous and controlled
- Steps should be quick without touching the hoop
- Maintain upright posture throughout the exercise

GROUP ACTIVITIES - HOOP

Activity 1: The group forms a circle, each member approximately 3 feet apart. Hold the hoop in front, both hands on top. On the count of "1, 2, 3," everyone passes their hoop to the person on their right by rolling it along the floor, then catching the hoop that was rolled to them. A rhythmic count should be achieved - 1, 2, 3, PASS, 1, 2, 3, PASS, and so on.

Activity 2: The group forms a circle, each person 1 foot apart. The hoops are held at the left side of the body. On the count of "1, 2, 3, STEP IN," everyone steps into the hoop with the left foot, bringing the hoop up over the head, down the right side of the body stepping out with the right foot, and hands the hoop to the class member on the right while accepting a new hoop from the left.

BALL - HOLD, BALANCE

The ball is held balanced on your open palm, without the fingers gripping the ball.

1 **Move Ball With Two Hands** The ball is held with two hands. Body remains stationary. The ball is moved from side to side, high and low, and near and far.

2 **Balance and Move** The ball is balanced on one hand, then the other hand. Move the ball from side to side, high and low, and near and far.

3 **Pendulum** Swing the ball with an extended arm using both the right and left hands.

4  **Pendulum With Knee Bends** Swing the ball with simultaneous bending of the knees using both the right and left hands.

5  **Body Circle** Circle the ball around the body, passing the ball from hand to hand.

6 **Swing and Chassé** Swing the ball, balanced on one hand with 4 chass(e) steps.

BALL - BOUNCING

1 **Bounce and Catch - Two Hands** Hold the ball with two hands, bounce once and catch, bounce four times and catch, bounce eight times and catch.

2 **Bounce and Catch - One Hand** Hold the ball with the right hand. Bounce eight times and catch. Repeat the activity with the left hand.

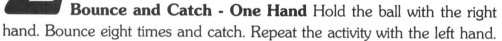

3 **Bounce and Walk** Bounce the ball eight times with the preferred hand while walking forward in a straight line. Catch the ball to finish.

What to Practice:
- Stretched arms should be relaxed
- Bouncing should be a gentle pushing motion, not a slapping action
- Maintain upright body while walking

SUPPLEMENTAL BALL ACTIVITIES

Activity 1: Partner Bounce and Catch Partners face each other standing approximately ten feet apart. The first partner performs eight right hand bounces with simultaneous knee bending, then places the ball on the palm of the hand, swings the straight arm once or twice and bounces the ball to the facing partner. Receiving the ball in two hands the second partner repeats the bouncing and returns the ball with a bounce. This is repeated by each partner on the left side.

What to Practice:
- Knee bending should be rhythmical
- Keep trunk upright throughout
- Bouncing should be a pushing, not slapping action
- Nestle ball in the palm of the hand
- Arm should be straight in the swing
- Release ball toward end of swing, follow through with the arm
- Arms should be outstretched to receive the ball

Activity 2: Bounce Across The ball is bounced from side to side across the body starting with a side lunge and rhythmically transferring the weight to a lunge on the opposite side in preparation for the catch. Repeat the activity four times.

Activity 3: Bounce Up and Down The ball is bounced with one hand while simultaneously jumping from two feet. Eight bounces with each hand are executed.

Activity 4: Change Height of Bounce Bounce the ball at different levels by changing body positions.

BALL - ROLLING

1 **Roll Under** Roll the ball under the leg, hand to hand, in a single kneeling position (one knee up).

2 **Roll and Retrieve** The ball is rolled along the floor, the performer travels ahead of the ball and retrieves it.

3 **Roll and Catch in a Balance** Retrieve the ball while various balances are held.

4 **Roll on Body Parts** Roll the ball on the legs from feet to hips, on the arms from hands to shoulders, or on the back from neck to bottom.

BALL - THROWING AND CATCHING

1 **Toss and Catch - Two Hands** The ball is thrown and caught using two hands from a kneeling position then a standing position. Repeat the activity four times.

2 **Toss and Catch - One Hand** Swing the ball backward with one hand while simultaneously bending the knees slightly, then swing it forward and execute a small toss of the ball while extending the legs. Catch the ball with the same hand. Repeat the activity with the other hand on the opposite side.

What to Practice:
- Maintain straight arm throughout
- Follow through arm action at release and catch
- Keep trunk upright throughout
- Make sure that your transitions between throwing and catching are smooth and continuous.

3 **Toss and Catch in a Series** A series of throws and catches are performed in kneeling and standing positions using only one hand.

4 **Gallop and Bounce** Initially the ball is in the palm of the hands and eight forward gallop steps are executed: four on the right, then four on the left. Four gallop steps with bounce are performed on each side. The preferred hand may be used for bouncing throughout.

What to Practice:
- Galloping action should be continuous
- Make sure bounce and gallop are coordinated
- Keep head and back up

SUPPLEMENTAL BALL ACTIVITY

Activity 1: Throw and Catch Behind

- How many ways can you throw?
- How many ways can you catch?
- How many different positions can you demonstrate while catching?
- How many different things can you do before catching? (run, jump, leap, turn, kick . . .)

RIBBON - SWINGS

Holding the Ribbon Stick The stick is held at the end, opposite the ribbon attachments. This end of the stick is placed near the base of the palm, the thumb and fingers are curled around the body of the stick with the index finger extended pointing along the shaft.

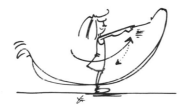

Technique: Holding the stick with a straight (extended) arm, swing the ribbon forward then backward, making an arc (or half circle) patterns.

Drills:
- Try swings with the left and right hands
- Try swings front and backwards
- Try swings from side to side
- Try swings overhead from side to side
- Try swings with body movements: while walking, with a chassé, with turns

RIBBON - LARGE CIRCLES

Technique: Holding the stick with a straight (extended) arm, circle the ribbon, forming a large pattern, by rotating the shoulder only. Try to keep the straight arm passing near the ear at the top and close to the leg at the bottom of the circle.

Drills:

- Try large circles clockwise and counter-clockwise
- Try large circles with the left and the right hand
- Try large circles over head and in front of the body
- Try large circles with body movements: Chassés, 360 degree turns, while walking and running in different directions, while kneeling and leaning to the side

---

Combinations: Try combining swings with large circle patterns. Then try combining swings with large circle patterns with body movements.

RIBBON - SNAKES

Technique 1: By holding the stick with a straight (extended) arm, move just the wrist in a small, side to side pattern. The wrist must move quickly to achieve this pattern.

Technique 2: By holding the stick with a straight (extended) arm, move just the wrist in a small up and down pattern while turning the body 360 degrees. The wrist must move quickly to achieve this pattern.

Drills:
- Try snakes with the left and right hands
- Try snakes moving the ribbon to the left and then to the right
- Try snakes overhead, moving from back to front
- Try snakes low to the ground while walking backwards
- Try snakes with chassés to the side ending with a 360 degree turn
- Try combining swings and large circle patterns with snake patterns
- Try swings, large circles, and snakes with different body movements

RIBBON - SPIRALS

Technique: By holding the stick with a straight (extended) arm, move only the wrist in a small, circular pattern as though you were stirring a pot with a spoon. The wrist must move quickly to achieve this pattern.

Drills:

- Try spirals with the left and with the right hand
- Try spirals moving the ribbon left to right and right to left
- Try spirals clockwise and counter-clockwise
- Try spirals while walking backwards
- Try spirals while walking backwards and holding the ribbon behind the body

Combinations:

- Try combining swings, large circle, snake, and spiral patterns
- Try combining swings, large circle, snake, and spiral patterns in conjunction with the body movements: chassés, kneeling, 360 degree turns, jumps, leaps, and arching positions
- Using music, combine the ribbon patterns with specific body movements into a short (30 second) routine.

Rhythmic Skills Checklists

ROPE	Date Skill Series Completed
Circling skills	
Overhead	
At the Side	
In Front	
Figure Eight	
Swinging skills	
Side to Side	
Front to Back	
Jumping and Hopping	
Jump on a Spot	
Hop, then Jump	
Traveling Hops and Pose	
Side to Side Jump	
Cross Over	
Group Activities with a Long Rope	
Double Turns	
Throwing and Catching	
Swing Out and Back	
Circle, Toss, and Catch	
Supplemental Rope Activities	
Balances and Poses	
Body Wrap	

HOOP	Date Skill Series Completed
Rolling	
Side to Side	
Lunge Roll	
Back Spinning	
Roll and Jump Over	
Backspin, Kick, and Catch	
Spinning	
Spin in Place	
Spin and Kick	
Spin in both Hands	
Spin and Run, Skip, or Jump	
Circling	
Circle on Both Arms	
Circle on One Hand	
Circle on One Hand and Walk	
Throwing and Catching	
Swing from One Hand to the Other	
Swing, Toss, and Catch	
Additional Throwing and Catching Activities	
Supplemental Hoop	
Activities Step In and Out (Side to Side)	
Step In and Out (Front and Back)	
Group Activities	
One	
Two	

BALL	Date Skill Series Completed
Hold and Balance	
Move Ball With Two Hands	
Balance and Move	
Pendulum	
Pendulum with Knee Bends	
Body Circle	
Swing and Chassé	
Bouncing	
Bounce and Catch - 2 Hands	
Bounce and Catch - 1 Hand	
Bounce and Walk	
Supplemental Ball Activities	
Partner Bounce and Catch	
Bounce Across	
Bounce Up and Down	
Change Height of Bounce	
Rolling	
Roll Under	
Roll and Retrieve	
Roll and Catch in a Balance	
Roll on Body Parts	
Throwing and Catching	
Toss and Catch - 2 Hands	
Toss and Catch - 1 Hand	
Toss and Catch in a Series	
Gallop and Bounce	
Supplemental Ball Activity	
Throw and Catch Behind	

RIBBON	Date Skill Series Completed
Swings	
Large Circles	
Snakes	
Spirals	

Glossary

BASIC BODY POSITIONS

Demi-plié : This is the position of the legs and feet used in preparation for jumps, turns, and in landings. Your knees are slightly flexed and turned out along with the feet.

Front Support: Any support position where your arms are straight and extended in front of your body.

Inverted: Any position in which your lower body is moved into a position above your upper body. (When you stand on your hands, you are *inverted.*)

Pike: Your body is flexed forward at the hips, while keeping the legs straight.

Prone: Lying face down with the body straight.

Rear Support: Any support position where your arms are straight and extended behind your body.

Squat: Support your body on the balls of the feet with the knees and hips flexed so that your seat is near, but not touching, your heels. Your torso is kept erect.

Straddle: A position in which your legs are straight and extended sideward.

Straight (Basic) Stand: Standing with your heels together, feet turned out (45 degrees), legs straight, and torso and head erect with your arms down at your sides.

Straight or Stretched (Layout): In the layout position, your body is straight and completely extended.

Supine: Lying flat on your back with the body straight.

Tuck: Your body is "curled up in a ball" when you are in the *tuck* position. The upper body is flexed forward, flexed at the hips, and the knees are flexed and pulled up to the chest.

JUMPS

Assemblé : Push upward off one foot, while swinging the other leg forward and upward, and bring your feet together upon landing.

Foutté : Push off one leg while kicking the other leg forward and upward while executing a 180 degree turn, and land on your take-off leg. Your other leg will remain extended rearward.

Hitchkick: Push upward off one leg while swinging the other leg forward and upward, switching legs in the air, and landing on the other foot, in a demi-plié.

Hop: Take off from one foot to land on the same foot.

Jump: Move from both feet to both feet.

Leap: Move from one foot to the other foot, showing flight.

Sissone: Step forward on one foot, bring the other foot forward to a position behind the first, jump and separate the legs to a split position, and land on the first leg.

Tourjeté : Push off one leg while kicking the other leg forward and upward executing a 180 degree turn, switch the legs in the air, and land on the first leg. Your take-off leg ends extended rearward.

PREPARATORY MOVEMENTS

Chassé : Step forward with one leg and spring slightly off the floor. Extend the legs and close them together. Land on the back leg with the front leg raised in preparation for the next skill.

A chassé can be performed in a forward or sideward direction.

Hurdle: A long, low, and powerful skip step, which may be preceded by one or more running steps.

Lunge: A lunge is a position in which one leg is flexed approximately 90 degrees, and your other leg is straight and extended. Your body is stretched and upright over the flexed leg.

HAND GRIPS

Overgrip: Grasping the bar with your thumbs pointing toward each other.

Undergrip: Grasping the bar with both of your thumbs facing out, away from each other.

Mixed grip: One hand in overgrip and the other in undergrip.

INVERTED SKILLS

Bridge: An arched position with your feet and hands flat on the floor and the abdomen up.

Cartwheel: The rhythm of the cartwheel is "hand, hand, foot, foot." Step forward with one foot, lift the other leg upward and backward while placing the hands onto the mat in front of the support leg. As the body becomes inverted, the legs remain in a straddled position (arms and legs look like the spokes of a wheel,) and land one foot at a time.

Handstand: Hands are flat on the floor, shoulder-width apart, and the body completely extended and straight, legs together.

Headstand: Place the hands and forehead on the floor in a triangular shape (head in front of hands), and extend the hips and legs straight upward over the triangular base of support.

Round-off: A round-off is a dynamic turning movement. Step forward and push off one leg while swinging the legs upward in a fast cartwheel type motion. As your body becomes inverted, execute a 90 degree turn, push off your hands, the legs are brought together just before landing. You should be facing the direction from which you started.

Tripod: Place the hands and forehead on the floor in a triangular shape (head in front of hands), and extend the hips above the triangular base. Your body is piked with the knees bent, resting on your elbows.

GENERAL TERMINOLOGY

Cast: From a front support (on uneven bars or horizontal bar) with your hands in overgrip. You will flex at the hips (90 degrees) and immediately thrust the legs backward and upward while maintaining the support position with extended arms.

Dismount: A skill you perform from the apparatus to a controlled landing on a mat.

Flank: A skill in which your body passes over a piece of equipment with the side of your body facing the apparatus.

Flexibility: The range of motion through which a body part, such as the shoulders or legs, can move without feeling pain.

Panel Mats: Basic mats which are constructed of a single layer of resilient foam, ranging in thickness from one to two inches, that can be folded into panels approximately two feet wide.

Pivot: A sharp 1/2 turn around a single point of support, like one hand.

Rear: A descriptive term indicating that the body passes over or around an apparatus with the back of the body leading or facing the apparatus.

Rebound: A quick jump using very little flexion of the hips, knees, or ankles.

Sequence: Two or more positions or skills which are performed together creating a different skill or activity.

Spot: To spot is to physically guide and/or assist a gymnast while performing a skill. Coaches spot for safety and when they are teaching new skills.

Spotting also refers to focusing the eyes on a particular point or place while performing a skill, such as to "spot" a turn.

Snap: A very quick movement of the body, usually from a 3/4 handstand position, moving the feet to the ground bringing the body to a near upright position.

Stick: A gymnast "sticks" a landing when he/she executes a landing with correct technique and no movement of the feet.

Wedge: A developmental mat filled with soft, shock absorbent foam. Its distinct shape is a sloping triangle with various heights and widths.

One of the most confusing areas of gymnastics can be the descriptions of starting and finishing positions of the gymnast. The following illustrations should help to increase your understanding.

Front or Frontways   **Rear or Rearways**

Front or **Frontways:** The gymnast faces the apparatus, with the line of the shoulders parallel to the apparatus — Front stand.

Rear or **Rearways:** The gymnast has the back toward the apparatus with the line of the shoulders parallel to the apparatus — Rear stand.

Side, Cross, Crossways

Side, Cross, Crossways: The gymnast has line of shoulders perpendicular to the apparatus. This is usually also indicated with Left or Right, Front or Back.